olive+oil

Jo McAuley

hamlyn

Notes

A few recipes include nuts or nut derivatives. It is advisable for those with known allergic reactions to nuts and nut derivatives and those who may be potentially vulnerable to these allergies, such as pregnant and nursing mothers, invalids, the elderly, babies and children, to avoid dishes made with nuts and nut oils. It is also prudent to check the labels of prepared ingredients for the possible inclusion of nut derivatives.

The Department of Health advises that eggs should not be consumed raw. This book contains some dishes made with raw or lightly cooked eggs. It is prudent for more vulnerable people such as pregnant and nursing mothers, invalids, the elderly, babies, and young children to avoid uncooked or lightly cooked dishes made with eggs.

Both metric and imperial measurements have been given. Use one set of measurements only, and not a mixture of both.

Standard level spoon measurements are used in all recipes: 1 tablespoon = one 15 ml spoon
1 teaspoon = one 5 ml spoon

Full-fat milk should be used unless otherwise stated. Fresh herbs should be used unless otherwise stated. Large eggs should be used unless otherwise stated.

Ovens should be preheated to the specified temperature – if using a fan-assisted oven, follow the manufacturer's instructions for adjusting the time and the temperature.

First published in Great Britain in 2005 by Hamlyn, a division of Octopus Publishing Group Ltd, 2–4 Heron Quays, London E14 4JP

Copyright © Octopus Publishing Group Ltd 2005

ISBN 0 600 61341 0
EAN 9780600613411

A CIP catalogue record for this book is available from the British Library

Printed and bound in China

10 9 8 7 6 5 4 3 2 1

contents

introduction

In many countries olives have been grown and used as a staple ingredient for hundreds of years, with preserved olives and bottles of olive oil taking pride of place in the kitchen and featuring somewhere in the majority of recipes. More recently, olives have found a following in non olive-producing countries and we're becoming more confident about using them in a variety of dishes. The olive really is quite special: its culinary uses are manifold, its flavour is rich and distinctive and its many health benefits proven. Over the following chapters, you'll find a selection of wonderfully diverse recipes with influences from around the world that also includes a number of gorgeous cakes and desserts. However, don't start cooking until you've discovered more about this truly versatile ingredient and how it is produced.

Olive trees thrive in a hot Mediterranean climate.

a place in history

The olive tree is believed to be one of the oldest cultivated trees in the world and there are countless references to it throughout history, particularly from the Mediterranean region, where both the fruit and the oil that it produced were a source of wealth and power. There is evidence that olive trees were grown on the island of Crete from as far back as 3,000 BC, having been introduced there from their native Asia. A regular feature of feasts, rites and religious ceremonies, the olive was revered for its health-giving properties and the oil was used to anoint everyone from priests and royalty to the newly born and the newly deceased in cultures and religions as diverse as the ancient world they inhabited. As armies marched, conquerors conquered and explorers wandered ever farther afield, the olive tree was scattered far and wide, and is grown today in parts of North America, South America and Australasia, as well as remaining a prominent feature of the Mediterranean landscape.

the olive branch

It is still countries in the Mediterranean region that produce the majority of the world's olives and olive oil. Spain is the largest olive oil producer, followed by Italy and then Greece, and, between them, these countries produce almost three-quarters of the world's supplies. Olives are an intrinsic part of the cuisine of most Mediterranean countries, with many dishes based around the flavours imparted by national and regional variations. Recipes such as Olive, Truffle and Ricotta Ravioli (page 38) and Whole Snapper with Roasted Mediterranean Vegetables (page 56) will give you an insight into some of the typical ingredients of this region, while demonstrating the cultural, as well as gastronomic, importance that the olive has maintained over the centuries. The Spanish took olive trees to America in the late 1700s and they flourished in the hot Californian climate, where they were cultivated to produce olive oil. Oil production is

Olives add depth of flavour to many different savoury dishes, while the oil is used in a wide variety of breads and desserts.

still concentrated here today, but it is a relatively small amount in proportion to consumption and most of America's olive oil is imported to keep up with the increasing demand. Fusion cuisine has evolved as ingredients from around the world have become more popular and readily available, and the olive is no exception.

from tree to table

Cultivation Olive trees love the sun and they can survive the hottest summer temperatures with very little water. However, they are adverse to the cold and a particularly harsh winter can ruin a potential crop. Far from being determined by different tree varieties, the colour of olives is actually solely due to their ripeness, with the fruit turning from green to purple, and then to black, as the ripening process advances.

Harvest time When it comes to harvesting, timing is everything: get it wrong and you may end up with olives that are low in quality and lacking in oil. The best time to harvest is when they are almost ripe, just before the acidity begins to increase. There are a number of ways in which olives can be harvested, but all of them are extremely labour-intensive. Picking them by hand is still considered to be the best way as it reduces the risk of the olives being damaged or bruised. Some producers have switched over to machine harvesting, but, as many olives are left behind, it still requires people to pick any remaining fruit by hand.

Pressing olives for oil If the harvested olives are to be used to produce olive oil, it's important that they are pressed as quickly as possible to ensure that the oil is of the highest quality. In fact, to be considered extra virgin oil (the highest quality and most expensive of the oils available), the olives must be pressed within 72 hours of harvesting. In an age of technological innovation, olive pressing for extra virgin oil remains staunchly traditional with no heat or chemical processes allowed, and a relatively simple revolving mill, which is used to crush the washed olives to a pulp. The oil that is extracted during this first cold pressing is what we know as virgin and extra virgin olive oil. To be extra virgin, the oil must have an acidity level of less than one per cent, whereas virgin olive oil will be of slightly higher acidity (between one and three per cent).

An astonishing 90 per cent of the oil is obtained from the olives during the first cold pressing and the pulp that is left behind is then sent to a refinery where it is exposed to heat and chemical processes in order to extract the remaining oil. This oil lacks the robust flavour of virgin olive oil and is simply referred to as olive oil.

There are literally hundreds of olive varieties, some of which are stuffed or flavoured with pimientos, garlic, anchovies, herbs or spices.

preserving olives

Olives can't be eaten straight from the tree; they have to be cured first and there are various ways of doing this, each varying in time and effort. As green olives are basically unripe, it's necessary to subject them to a process called lye curing before they can be preserved or pickled. This involves soaking them in a mixture of water and a substance called lye for about four days, changing the water a number of times each day. Black olives don't require this stage and they can be preserved immediately after harvesting. The most common curing or pickling substances are water, brine or oil. The longer the olives are cured, the better they will taste – if they're eaten too soon, they tend to be quite bitter.

to name but a few

If you thought that there were only two types of olive – green and black – then think again! With the flavour of the olive dependent on factors such as soil, climate, geographical location and harvesting methods, there are literally hundreds of variations, with flavours differing between regions in the same country and even between neighbouring farms, in the same way that wines from different vineyards vary. Such subtle nuances in taste might be discernible only to a real connoisseur; however, there are many varieties of olive that

are quite distinctive, due to their size, the ripeness at which they're picked and the curing process. Here are just a few:

Kalamata This is a well-known Greek black variety that has a rich colour and flavour.

Niçoise Served in the salad of the same name, this French variety is a black olive that's small in size, but big on flavour.

Manzanilla This is a Spanish green olive that's cured in brine. You'll often get a bowl of these if you're in a tapas bar.

Liguria This is an Italian black olive that packs a punch. It's also brine-cured.

Gaeto This is an Italian black olive that's dry-cured in salt.

a healthy option

The Mediterranean diet is often cited as being healthy, and low incidences of heart disease and a long life expectancy appear to back up this claim. A combination of factors such as a more active lifestyle and a diet rich in grains, fresh fruit, vegetables and fish are thought to be the reason, although it has in part been attributed to the consumption of olive oil – from eating the fruit itself and using olive oil when cooking. Despite having a high fat content, olive oil doesn't contain the saturated fats that are detrimental to cholesterol levels and is instead made up of monounsaturated fats. It is also believed to be beneficial for both the skin and hair, and the antioxidants it contains can help to fight common diseases such as cancer. It has also been suggested that olive oil might have a part to play in reducing the risk of developing rheumatoid arthritis.

storage and use

As they're preserved, olives will keep for anything up to 1½ years if they're unopened and the seal of the container hasn't been broken. Once opened, it's best to keep olives in their preserving liquid, either in the original jar or transferred to a bowl and covered. You should store opened olives in the refrigerator, where they'll keep for a couple of weeks. Olives are quite robust and can cope with high heats and extended cooking times, which makes them suitable for all kinds of recipes. Add whole black olives to casseroles and chunky pasta sauces – they'll become really tender and will impart a subtle flavour to the whole dish as well as releasing oil, which will add richness. Black olives will often have their stones left in and it's fine to cook them like this, but just make sure you remind your guests, so no one chips a tooth when they're eating!

Olives make a great snack or accompaniment to drinks, and what could be easier than filling a couple of bowls with a selection of green and black olives? This is where stuffed and flavoured varieties really come into their own and you'll be able to find these at food markets, delicatessens and larger supermarkets, with chilli, garlic, lemon, anchovies and rosemary being just some of the more popular flavourings. They also work well as part of a starter for a dinner party, almost like a mezze. Just fill the centre of the table with dishes of olives, hummus and cubes of feta cheese and accompany them with a selection of breads, such as pitta and ciabatta, warmed and cut into strips. It's a very sociable way of eating and not too time-consuming for the hosts! Other quick ideas for olives include chopping and scattering them over salads or sandwiches; whizzing them in a food processor (stones removed) to make a paste to rub over chicken and fish; using them as part of a pizza topping; or slicing them and adding to pasta sauces.

The colour of olive oil varies greatly depending on the country of origin.

dressings,
oils, sauces
and marinades

winter squash, bacon and olive sauce

1 kg (2 lb) butternut squash, peeled and
   cut into 2.5 cm (1 inch) chunks
4–5 garlic cloves
4 tablespoons extra virgin olive oil
½ teaspoon crushed chilli flakes
350 g (11½ oz) penne
2 tablespoons pine nuts
150 g (5 oz) piece of smoked bacon,
   diced
50 g (2 oz) mixed, stuffed, spicy-
   marinated olives, roughly chopped
1 roasted pepper, cut into strips
   (optional)
200 ml (7 fl oz) crème fraîche
salt and pepper
deep-fried sage leaves, to garnish
freshly grated Parmesan cheese,
   to serve

Serves 4
Preparation time: 12 minutes
Cooking time: 45 minutes

Combine these easily prepared ingredients with penne pasta and you have the perfect comfort dish for winter!

1 Toss the butternut squash and garlic cloves in 3 tablespoons of the olive oil, add the chilli flakes and season with salt and pepper. Tip into a large roasting tin and bake in a preheated oven, 190°C (375°F), Gas Mark 5, for 45 minutes until the squash is soft and golden.

2 Meanwhile, cook the pasta in a large pan of lightly salted boiling water for 10–12 minutes, or according to packet instructions. Drain well.

3 While the pasta is cooking, heat the remaining oil in a frying pan and fry the pine nuts over a low heat, moving them quickly around the pan, until they are golden brown. Drain on kitchen paper. Add the bacon and fry gently until it is golden and crispy. Add the olives and pepper, if using, and warm through for 2–3 minutes.

4 When the squash is cooked, toss it with the pine nuts, bacon, olives and roasted pepper, if using, and stir in the crème fraîche. Serve immediately with the pasta scattered with deep-fried sage leaves and a bowl of freshly grated Parmesan.

broad bean, prosciutto and mint pasta sauce

350 g (11½ oz) fusilli
250 g (8 oz) shelled baby broad beans
4–6 tablespoons extra virgin olive oil
rind of 1 lemon
175 g (6 oz) prosciutto, shredded
3–4 spring onions, finely sliced
8–10 mint leaves, shredded
125 g (4 oz) buffalo mozzarella, diced
salt

Serves 4
Preparation time: 8 minutes
Cooking time: 10–12 minutes

This is a good example of how many Italian pasta recipes use olive oil almost more as a dressing than a sauce, so that it just delicately coats the pasta.

1 Cook the pasta in a large pan of lightly salted boiling water for 10–12 minutes, or according to packet instructions. Drain well.

2 Meanwhile, bring a pan of salted water to the boil and cook the broad beans for 2–3 minutes. Drain the beans quickly and toss them in the oil with the lemon rind, prosciutto, spring onions and mint leaves.

3 Toss the freshly cooked pasta and the sauce together, then tip on to warm serving dishes. Scatter with the mozzarella and serve immediately.

pesto sauce with green olives

350 g (11½ oz) spaghetti or linguine

1 small garlic clove, peeled

25 g (1 oz) shelled walnuts

100 g (3½ oz) pitted green olives

large bunch of basil, leaves stripped,
plus extra for serving

3–4 tablespoons extra virgin olive oil

1 tablespoon lemon juice

50 g (2 oz) pecorino or Parmesan
cheese, finely grated, plus extra for
serving (optional)

salt and pepper

Serves 4
Preparation time: 7 minutes
Cooking time: 10–12 minutes

1 Cook the pasta in a large pan of lightly salted boiling water for 10–12 minutes, or according to packet instructions. Drain well.

2 Meanwhile, put the garlic, walnuts and olives in a food processor and process until finely chopped. Add the basil leaves and olive oil and blend until smooth.

3 Scrape the sauce into a bowl, stir in the lemon juice and pecorino or Parmesan, and season to taste with salt and pepper.

4 Toss the spaghetti or linguine in the pesto. Serve immediately with basil leaves and extra cheese, if desired.

tapenade dressing

100 g (3½ oz) pitted black olives, chopped

6 anchovies in olive oil, drained and chopped

2 tablespoons caperberries

50 g (2 oz) canned tuna in olive oil, drained

1 garlic clove, crushed

1 tablespoon chopped oregano

150 ml (¼ pint) extra virgin olive oil

2 tablespoons lemon juice

salt and pepper

Serves 4
Preparation time: 7 minutes

This Provençal dip makes an excellent simple dressing for robust salad leaves or roasted vegetables. It can also be spread on bread or toast or mixed with the yolks and used to stuff hard-boiled eggs.

1 Put the olives, anchovies, caperberries and tuna in a food processor and pulse briefly. Add the garlic and oregano and continue pulsing until you have a fairly smooth paste. With the machine running, pour in the oil and lemon juice in an even stream until it is completely incorporated.

2 Scrape the mixture into a bowl, season to taste with salt and pepper and serve as a dressing.

blue cheese and black olive dressing

1 shallot, preferably purple, very finely chopped

75 g (3 oz) blue cheese, such as Roquefort, crumbled

50 ml (2 fl oz) extra virgin olive oil

50 g (2 oz) pitted black olives, chopped

2 tablespoons chopped chives

2 tablespoons crème fraîche

freshly ground mixed peppercorns

salt

Serves 4
Preparation time: 5 minutes

Drizzle this dressing over grilled chicken or pork and serve with crusty bread to mop up the juices.

Whisk together all the ingredients in a bowl, season to taste with salt and pepper and serve immediately.

sun-dried tomato and olive dressing

8 sun-dried tomatoes in oil, drained and
   chopped
grated rind of ½ lemon
6 basil leaves, shredded
1 teaspoon grated fresh root ginger
½ teaspoon fennel seeds
¼ teaspoon paprika
6 tablespoons extra virgin olive oil
2 tablespoons sherry vinegar
salt and pepper

Serves 4
Preparation time: 5 minutes

This sultry dressing is a perfect partner for cold pasta salads or drizzled over freshly cooked fish.

Place all the ingredients in a jar, screw the lid on tightly and shake well to combine. Season to taste with salt and pepper and serve immediately.

real ranch dressing

2 tablespoons soured cream
100 ml (3½ fl oz) buttermilk
1 tablespoon red wine vinegar
1 garlic clove, crushed
1 teaspoon Worcestershire sauce
50 g (2 oz) pitted queen green olives,
   chopped
1 teaspoon extra virgin olive oil
1 tablespoon chopped dill
½ small onion, finely grated
salt and pepper

Serves 4
Preparation time: 7 minutes

This dressing is ideal with a baked potato and T-bone steak in true cowboy style.

Whisk together all the dressing ingredients in a bowl, season with salt and pepper and serve immediately.

flavoured oils

Use the same basic method to make all of these oils, just varying the flavouring ingredients. The golden rule is always to use the best oil you can find.

Pour 500 ml (17 fl oz) extra virgin olive oil into a saucepan and heat very gently with your chosen set of flavourings. The idea is just to warm the oil, not to get it hot. Remove the pan from the heat and leave it to cool completely, then pour the oil and the flavourings into a 600 ml (1 pint) bottle. Leave the bottle to stand in a cool place for at least 2 weeks before using. The Garlic and Saffron Oil, Lemon Grass, Ginger and Lime Leaf Oil and Mandarin and Lemon Oil all contain fresh ingredients, so they must be strained after 2 weeks to prevent harmful bacteria from growing. They can then be poured into clean bottles and kept, like the other oils, for up to 6 months.

smoky chipotle chilli and peppercorn oil

15 chipotle chillies, slightly crushed
2 tablespoons mixed peppercorns

Use this oil to drizzle over freshly cooked pizzas. The chillies give it a bit of a kick, so try a little before you completely cover your food.

juniper berry and bay leaf oil

1 tablespoon juniper berries
3 dried bay leaves

This is a decadent oil to drizzle over any game dish. The interesting flavours also make it ideal for using in sauces and dips.

garlic and saffron oil

10–12 garlic cloves, peeled
1 teaspoon saffron threads

This oil is perfect for making quick and interesting Italian bruschettas. Using a good quality oil and bread means that this is all you need for a delicious party nibble.

cumin, coriander and cardamom oil

1 tablespoon cumin seeds
1 tablespoon coriander seeds
10 green cardamom pods, crushed

No home-cooked Indian dish is complete without this authentically flavoured oil. It would work particularly well in chana masala or for pouring over dhal.

lemon grass, ginger and lime leaf oil

2 lemon grass stalks, peeled and sliced
50 g (2 oz) piece of fresh root ginger,
    unpeeled but thinly sliced
4–5 kaffir lime leaves, shredded

Bring some Far Eastern flavours into your kitchen with this exotic oil. This oil could be used on its own as a dipping sauce with some warm Lebanese bread.

mandarin and lemon oil

rind of 3 mandarin oranges
rind of 2 lemons, peeled with a
    vegetable peeler
1 cinnamon stick

Serving just a dash of this oil over a bowl of fresh strawberries will stop you ever wanting cream again! The fruity citrus kick is pleasantly surprising – try adding it to pasta salads too.

spanish marinade with chicken

Marinade:
250 ml (8 fl oz) full-fat natural yogurt
1 teaspoon smoked paprika
grated rind and juice of 1 lemon
1 tablespoon red wine vinegar
1 small onion, finely grated
2 garlic cloves, crushed
2 tablespoons chopped parsley, plus
    extra for serving
salt and pepper

1 large, free-range chicken, about
    1.8 kg (4 lb)
4 tablespoons Spanish extra virgin
    olive oil

Serves 4
Preparation time: 12 minutes, plus
    marinating and resting
Cooking time: 1½ hours

This marinade with its typically Spanish flavours of garlic, lemon and paprika is equally good with lamb. Ask your butcher to butterfly the leg of lamb for you.

1 Mix together all the marinade ingredients and season with salt and pepper. Rub this marinade very thoroughly into the skin of the chicken. Drizzle the olive oil over the chicken and leave to marinate in the refrigerator for at least 2 hours, but preferably overnight.

2 Transfer the chicken to a roasting tray and cook in a preheated oven, 180°C (350°F), Gas Mark 4, for 1½ hours.

3 Put the chicken on a warm plate, cover with foil and leave to rest in a warm place for about 10 minutes before carving.

barbecue marinade with chicken

2 tablespoons tomato ketchup

2 tablespoons Smoky Chipotle Chilli and
   Peppercorn Oil (see page 19)

3 tablespoons maple syrup

2 teaspoons grated fresh root ginger

1 large garlic clove, crushed

1 teaspoon ground cumin

1 teaspoon ground coriander

1 teaspoon dried oregano

50 ml (2 fl oz) fresh orange juice

1 tablespoon soy sauce

2 teaspoons Worcestershire sauce

1 teaspoon Tabasco sauce

4 boneless chicken breasts, with skin on

Serves 4

Preparation time: 15 minutes, plus
   cooling and marinating

Cooking time: about 15 minutes

1 Combine all the marinade ingredients in a small saucepan and place over a
   low heat. Bring slowly to the boil, then reduce the heat and simmer gently for
   2–3 minutes. Remove the pan from the heat and leave to cool.

2 Make 3 deep slashes in the chicken breasts using a sharp knife and work the
   cold marinade into the flesh. Cover and leave to marinate for 1 hour, then cook
   the chicken on a prepared barbecue or under a preheated hot grill for about
   8–10 minutes, turning it once, until it is browned and completely cooked through.

lime, coriander and chilli-spiked marinade with tiger prawns

finely grated rind of 2 limes
2 kaffir lime leaves, crushed
1 small bunch of coriander, roughly chopped, plus extra sprigs to serve
1 tablespoon grated fresh ginger
2 red chillies, finely sliced
1 tablespoon Thai fish sauce
4 tablespoons Lemon Grass, Ginger and Lime Leaf Oil (see page 19)
2 teaspoons rice vinegar
500 g (1 lb) raw tiger prawns, in their shells

To serve:
steamed rice
1 lime, sliced

Serves 4
Preparation time: 12 minutes, plus marinating
Cooking time: 3–5 minutes

1 Put all the marinade ingredients in a bowl and mix until well combined. Brush over the prawns, then cover and leave to marinate for 30–60 minutes.

2 Heat a large saucepan of water and place a bamboo steamer on top. Arrange the prawns in the steamer, cover with a lid and leave to steam for 3–5 minutes until the prawns are cooked.

3 Serve the prawns with plain steamed rice, garnished with coriander sprigs and a slice of lime.

sides and
starters

olive focaccia with tomato and parmesan salad

7 g (¼ oz) packet fast-action dried yeast
300 g (10 oz) plain white flour
1 teaspoon salt
½ teaspoon caster sugar
200 ml (7 fl oz) warm water
5 tablespoons extra virgin olive oil
semolina, for dusting
100 g (3½ oz) mixed marinated olives
2 shallots, halved and very finely sliced
2 garlic cloves, finely chopped
small bunch of shredded basil leaves
1 tablespoon coarse sea salt

Tomato and Parmesan salad:
50 g (2 oz) Parmesan cheese shavings
2 really red Italian plum tomatoes,
   sliced
150 g (5 oz) cherry tomatoes, halved
2 yellow tomatoes, sliced
5–6 large basil leaves, torn
4 tablespoons extra virgin olive oil
2 tablespoons reduced balsamic
   vinegar

Serves 4–6
Preparation time: 35 minutes,
   plus proving
Cooking time: 25–30 minutes

1 Put the yeast, flour, salt and sugar in a large bowl and stir together. Make a well in the centre and pour in the warm water and 2–3 tablespoons of the olive oil. Stir the mixture to incorporate all the dry ingredients from the side of the bowl until you have a soft, sticky dough.

2 Transfer the dough to a lightly floured surface and knead it for at least 10 minutes, adding more flour if necessary, until the dough is smooth and elastic – it is ready when a finger mark springs back.

3 Put the dough in a large, oiled bowl and cover it loosely with oiled clingfilm. Set aside in a warm place for about 1 hour until doubled in size.

4 Punch the dough to release the air, then put it on a lightly floured surface. Push it into a rectangular shape, about 25 x 20 cm (10 x 8 inches), then put it on a baking sheet dusted with semolina. Make indentations all over the surface of the bread with your fingers, then cover the bread with oiled clingfilm and leave to rise again for another hour.

5 Gently scatter the bread with the marinated olives, shallots, garlic and basil leaves, taking care not to let the dough collapse. Drizzle with the remaining 2–3 tablespoons olive oil, sprinkle with half the sea salt and bake in a preheated oven, 200°C (400°F), Gas Mark 6, for 25–30 minutes until golden and crusty. Sprinkle the focaccia with the remaining salt and allow it to cool slightly.

6 To make the salad, scatter the Parmesan shavings over a large plate and arrange the tomatoes and basil leaves over the top. Drizzle with the olive oil and balsamic vinegar and serve immediately with the olive focaccia.

olive breadsticks with artichoke and almond paste

1 teaspoon fast-action dried yeast
175 g (6 oz) rye flour
1 teaspoon salt, plus extra to sprinkle
½ teaspoon dark brown sugar
1 tablespoon extra virgin olive oil, plus
    extra for drizzling
100 ml (3½ fl oz) warm water
1 tablespoon green olive paste

Green olive, artichoke and almond paste:
100 g (3½ oz) almond-stuffed green olives
100 g (3½ oz) drained cooked artichoke
    hearts in olive oil
3 tablespoons extra virgin olive oil, plus
    extra for serving
100 g (3½ oz) mild, soft goats' cheese
½ teaspoon chilli flakes (optional)
½ teaspoon caraway seeds

Serves 4
Preparation time: 30 minutes,
    plus proving
Cooking time: 10 minutes

Stuffed olives have a longer history than you might expect. As long ago as the 18th century, producers in Aix-en-Provence were pitting their olives and stuffing them with anchovies, capers and tuna.

1 Put the yeast, flour, salt and sugar in a mixing bowl and stir together, then pour in the olive oil, warm water and olive paste. Mix well until combined then tip the dough on to a floured surface and knead into a soft ball. Knead the dough for about 10 minutes until smooth and elastic, using more flour if necessary. Place in an oiled bowl, cover loosely with oiled clingfilm and set aside in a warm place for about 1 hour until doubled in size.

2 Punch the dough to release the air, then tear off small balls about the size of a small walnut and roll them into long, thin strips. Don't worry about getting them perfectly straight and smooth – the roughness is part of their charm. You should be able to make about 20. Put them on lightly oiled baking sheets, giving them room to spread a little, cover loosely with oiled clingfilm again and leave to rise again for another 30 minutes.

3 Sprinkle the breadsticks with a little extra sea salt and bake in a preheated oven, 200°C (400°F), Gas Mark 6, for about 10 minutes until dry and crisp. Cool on a wire rack.

4 To make the dipping paste, tip the olives, artichokes and olive oil into a food processor or liquidizer and whizz until almost smooth. Add the goats' cheese and pulse until combined, then stir in the chilli flakes, if using, and the caraway seeds. Scrape the paste into a bowl and drizzle with some extra olive oil. Serve with the olive breadsticks.

warm spinach and chorizo salad with poached quails' eggs

3 tablespoons Spanish extra virgin
  olive oil
200 g (7 oz) medium-hot chorizo
  sausage, thickly sliced
1 small red onion, cut into wedges
1 garlic clove, chopped
1 teaspoon smoked paprika
1 teaspoon dried oregano
8–12 quails' eggs
300 g (10 oz) baby spinach leaves,
  washed and dried
1 tablespoon aged sherry vinegar
1 tablespoon salted capers, well rinsed,
  or capers in brine, drained
2 tablespoons chopped chives

Serves 4
Preparation time: 15 minutes
Cooking time: 15–20 minutes

The heat and dryness of the Spanish climate result in an olive oil that is smooth, golden, fruity and aromatic – making it a natural choice for the other Spanish ingredients in this recipe.

1 Heat 1 tablespoon of the olive oil in a large frying pan over a moderately high heat. Add the sliced chorizo and fry for about 3 minutes until crisp and golden. Add the red onion and garlic and continue cooking for 2 minutes until the onion is wilted and coloured but not completely soft. Stir in the paprika and oregano and remove from the heat.

2 Bring a small pan of water to a gentle simmering point. Crack a quail's egg into a small saucer, then drop it carefully into the simmering water. Leave for 1 minute, then remove with a slotted spoon and place on kitchen paper. Keep the egg warm while you poach the remaining eggs.

3 Stir the spinach leaves quickly into the chorizo mixture with the remaining olive oil and the sherry vinegar. Arrange on serving plates, scatter with the capers and top with 2–3 quails' eggs. Sprinkle the eggs with the chives and serve immediately.

smoked taramasalata with raw vegetables

50 g (2 oz) stale bread, soaked in 75 ml (3 fl oz) cold milk
100 g (3½ oz) smoked cod's roe
3 tablespoons lemon juice
1 small garlic clove, crushed
150 ml (¼ pint) extra virgin olive oil
3 tablespoons Greek yogurt
salt and pepper

To serve:
selection of raw vegetables, such as radishes and baby carrots
black Greek olives
hot griddled pittas

Serves 4
Preparation time: 15 minutes

This Greek dip is a favourite worldwide. Traditionally, it was made with the smoked roe of grey mullet, but smoked cod's roe is widely used today.

1 Squeeze the excess milk from the bread. Put it into a food processor with the cod's roe, lemon juice and crushed garlic and pulse until smooth. With the machine running, very slowly drizzle the olive oil into the cod's roe paste until it is all completely incorporated. If the mixture seems a little thick, add 1–2 tablespoons boiling water and pulse quickly.

2 Scrape the taramasalata into a dish and stir in the Greek yogurt and salt and pepper to taste. Serve with raw vegetables, black olives and hot griddled pittas.

hot and smoky hummus with warm flatbread

400 g (13 oz) can cooked chickpeas,
    drained
3 tablespoons lemon juice
1 large garlic clove, crushed
2 tablespoons light tahini
1 teaspoon hot smoked paprika, plus
    extra for sprinkling
½ teaspoon ground cumin
150 ml (¼ pint) extra virgin olive oil, plus
    extra for drizzling
2 tablespoons sesame seeds
salt and pepper

To serve:
4 sheets of Lebanese or Turkish
    flatbread
crunchy raw vegetables (optional)

Serves 4
Preparation time: 12 minutes
Cooking time: 20 minutes

Lebanese flatbread is a round, flat, slightly puffy bread, which goes very well with mezze dips. If you can't get hold of it, pittas or even soft flour tortillas would make a good substitute.

1 Put all the ingredients except the olive oil and sesame seeds in a food processor and blend until smooth. With the machine still running, very slowly drizzle the olive oil into the chickpea paste until it is all completely incorporated. Season with salt and pepper and scrape into a small dish.

2 Heat a dry, nonstick frying pan and toast the sesame seeds over a moderately low heat, moving them quickly around the pan until they are golden brown. Stir most of the sesame seeds into the hummus and sprinkle the rest over the top.

3 Wrap the flatbread in foil and heat in a preheated oven, 160°C (325°F), Gas Mark 3, for 20 minutes until warmed through. Drizzle the hummus with olive oil, sprinkle with paprika and serve with the warm flatbread and crunchy vegetables, if liked.

black and green marinated olives

Black olives:
150 g (5 oz) small black dry-cured
　　Provençal olives
2 bay leaves
1 teaspoon fennel seeds
1 teaspoon dried thyme
1 teaspoon dried oregano
1 small dried chilli
1 teaspoon coriander seeds
finely grated rind of 1 small orange
extra virgin olive oil

Green olives:
150 g (5 oz) fat green Spanish olives
1 teaspoon cumin seeds
1 teaspoon coriander seeds
½ teaspoon peppercorns
2 garlic cloves, peeled but left whole
¼ preserved lemon, finely chopped
1 tablespoon sherry vinegar
1 dried rosemary sprig
extra virgin olive oil

To garnish:
fennel sprigs (optional)
spicy toasted nuts (optional)

Serves 4
Preparation time: 15 minutes
Cooking time: 2–3 minutes

Marinating ready-cured olives using the traditional flavourings given here is both quick and simple. You can also pit ready-cured olives and stuff them with anchovies, pimientos or blanched almonds, although this is a rather fiddly job.

1 Put the green and black olives in separate freezer bags and tap them gently with a rolling pin to crack them open a little.

2 Tip the black olives into a dish and add all the remaining ingredients. Mix until well combined, then tip the mixture into a 250 ml (8 fl oz) sterilized jar. Top up with olive oil and screw the lid on tightly.

3 To make the green olives, heat a small, dry frying pan and toast the cumin and coriander seeds and peppercorns over a moderate heat until the seeds begin to pop and release an aromatic smell. Put the green olives in a bowl with the garlic cloves, preserved lemon and sherry vinegar and stir in the toasted seeds and peppercorns. Tip into a 250 ml (8 fl oz) sterilized jar, pushing the rosemary sprig into the jar at the same time, and top up with olive oil, covering all the ingredients completely. Screw the lid on tightly.

4 Store the olives in a cool, dark place for at least a week. Serve them as part of a tapas starter garnished with fennel sprigs or as a canapé with spicy toasted nuts.

calamari with lemon and herb mayonnaise

Lemon and herb mayonnaise:
2 egg yolks
½ teaspoon wholegrain mustard
1 tablespoon lemon juice, plus extra
   to taste
200 ml (7 fl oz) light olive oil
1 tablespoon chopped flat leaf parsley
1 tablespoon chopped chervil
1 tablespoon chopped chives
2 tablespoons chopped watercress
finely grated rind of 1 lemon
1 small garlic clove, crushed
salt and pepper

500 g (1 lb) prepared squid
50 g (2 oz) plain flour
1 tablespoon paprika
pinch of cayenne pepper
olive oil, for deep-frying
salt and pepper

To serve:
chopped parsley
coarse sea salt (optional)
lemon wedges

Serves 4
Preparation time: 30 minutes
Cooking time: 9 minutes

1 To make the mayonnaise, beat the egg yolks in a bowl with the mustard and lemon juice. Gradually add the olive oil, drop by drop, beating constantly, until it is all completely incorporated and you have a thick, smooth emulsion. Season with salt and pepper and stir in the herbs, lemon rind and garlic, adding a little extra lemon juice to taste. Cover and place in the refrigerator until required.

2 Wash the squid and pat dry with kitchen paper, then cut the bodies into rings about 1.5 cm (¼ inch) thick. Mix together the flour, paprika and cayenne and season well with salt and pepper. Place in a plastic bag, add the squid rings and tentacles and shake well until they are completely coated.

3 Heat the oil in a large frying pan or deep-fat fryer to 180°C (350°F) or until a cube of bread browns in 20 seconds. Remove about a third of the squid from the bag and shake off any excess flour. Carefully drop the squid into the hot oil and fry for 2–3 minutes until golden and crispy, then remove with a slotted spoon. Drain the squid on kitchen paper and keep them warm while you cook the rest.

4 Divide the calamari among 4 small bowls, sprinkle with parsley, and sea salt if using, and serve immediately with lemon wedges and a dollop of mayonnaise.

charred artichoke, olive and parma ham tartlets

4 small marinated artichoke hearts,
   halved
1 tablespoon olive oil
12 thin slices of Parma ham
4 large free-range eggs
125 g (4 oz) ricotta cheese
50 g (2 oz) pitted black olives, roughly
   chopped
2–3 spring onions, thinly sliced
½ tablespoon chopped chives
1 tablespoon chopped basil
½ tablespoon chopped tarragon
salt and pepper

To garnish:
shredded basil leaves
toasted hazelnuts

Serves 4
Preparation time: 25 minutes
Cooking time: 22–27 minutes

The little marinated artichoke halves sold in Italian delicatessens are perfect for this recipe, but if you cannot find them, use canned artichoke hearts instead.

1 Heat a griddle pan over a moderately high heat and brush the halved artichoke hearts all over with the olive oil. When the pan is hot, put the artichoke hearts, cut side down, in the pan and leave to char for about 2 minutes. Turn off the heat, use tongs to remove the artichokes and put them cut-side up on a plate. Set aside.

2 Cut 4 of the Parma ham slices into thin shreds and cut the remaining slices in half. Use the halved slices to line 8 moulds of a muffin tin.

3 Lightly beat the eggs in a large bowl, then beat in the ricotta until smooth. Stir in the olives, spring onions, chives, basil, tarragon and shredded ham and season well with pepper and a pinch of salt.

4 Carefully divide the egg mixture among the 8 muffin moulds – they should all be about two-thirds full. Place an artichoke half, cut-side up, in the centre of each tartlet, so that the charred side is showing.

5 Bake the tartlets in a preheated oven, 200°C (400°F), Gas Mark 6, for 20–25 minutes until they are golden and firm to the touch. Remove the tartlets from the oven and leave to cool in the tin for a few minutes. Carefully remove the tartlets from the tin and serve garnished with shredded basil leaves and sprinkled with a few chopped, toasted hazelnuts.

carpaccio with red onion and olive dressing

1 tablespoon mixed peppercorns
1 tablespoon Sichuan peppercorns
1 teaspoon coriander seeds
475 g (15 oz) beef fillet
50 ml (2 fl oz) extra virgin olive oil
75 g (3 oz) lambs' lettuce
small handful of cress
100 g (3½ oz) small black olives in
    olive oil
1 small red onion, halved and very
    finely sliced
½ tablespoon soft green peppercorns
25 g (1 oz) peppery pecorino cheese,
    shaved using a vegetable peeler
3 tablespoons balsamic vinegar

Serves 4
Preparation time: 25 minutes,
    plus freezing
Cooking time: about 5 minutes

1 Put the mixed and Sichuan peppercorns and coriander seeds into a mortar and pound with a pestle until they are coarsely ground. Sprinkle the mixture evenly over a large plate or a chopping board.

2 Rub the beef fillet with 1 tablespoon of the olive oil, then roll it over the pepper mix until the surface is completely encrusted.

3 Heat a dry frying pan until it is very hot and quickly sear the beef fillet, turning it frequently, for about 5 minutes until it is blackened all over. Remove the beef from the heat, wrap it tightly in foil and put it in the freezer for about 1 hour.

4 When the beef is firm and beginning to freeze, remove it from the freezer and put it on a chopping board. Using a very sharp knife, slice the meat as thinly as possible – it should be in wafer-thin slices. Arrange the slices in a single layer on 4 large serving plates and put the lambs' lettuce, cress and black olives on top. Scatter with the red onion slices, green peppercorns and pecorino. Cover lightly and set aside until the beef reaches room temperature. Just before serving, drizzle the beef with the remaining olive oil and the balsamic vinegar.

antipasti of baba ganoush and skorthalia with crostini

Baba ganoush:
8 tablespoons Greek extra virgin
  olive oil, plus extra for drizzling
425 g (14 oz) aubergine, cut into large
  chunks
4–5 large garlic cloves, peeled
2 tablespoons Greek yogurt
2–3 tablespoons lemon juice
½ teaspoon ground cumin
2 tablespoons chopped parsley
1 tablespoon tahini

Skorthalia:
100 g (3½ oz) slightly stale sourdough or
  other rustic bread
3–4 garlic cloves, crushed
1 teaspoon coarse sea salt
75 g (3 oz) shelled walnuts, roughly
  chopped
150 ml (¼ pint) Greek extra virgin
  olive oil, plus extra for drizzling
3 tablespoons lemon juice
salt and pepper

Crostini:
1 demi-baguette, cut into thin slices
salt

Serves 4
Preparation time: 25 minutes
Cooking time: about 1 hour

Roasting the garlic alongside the aubergine gives it a slightly sweeter, earthier taste, which contrasts well with the sharp strength of the raw garlic in the skorthalia. Try to use a good, peppery Greek olive oil for both these mezze dishes.

1 To make the baba ganoush, put 4 tablespoons of the olive oil in a bowl, add the aubergine and garlic and toss well. Transfer to a roasting tin and bake in a preheated oven, 200°C (400°F), Gas Mark 6, for about 45 minutes until they are soft and lightly charred. Allow to cool. Reduce the oven to 190°C (375°F), Gas Mark 5.

2 Scrape the aubergine and garlic into a food processor and add the yogurt, lemon juice, cumin, parsley and tahini. Whizz until blended but not completely smooth. Cover and set aside.

3 To make the skorthalia, soak the bread in hot water for 30 seconds. Squeeze it dry and put in a large mortar with the garlic, sea salt and walnuts. Pound with a pestle until a smooth, thick paste forms. Add the olive oil, a little at a time, and continue to pound until it is all completely incorporated. Stir in the lemon juice and season to taste with salt and pepper.

4 Cut the demi-baguette into thin slices and arrange them on a baking sheet. Drizzle with the remaining 4 tablespoons of olive oil and sprinkle with salt, then bake in the preheated oven for about 12 minutes until golden and crisp. Remove the crostini from the oven and keep warm.

5 Serve both dishes in small bowls drizzled with extra olive oil and accompanied by the warm crostini.

olive, truffle and ricotta ravioli

Pasta:
200 g (7 oz) type 00 pasta flour
2 large eggs, lightly beaten
salt

Filling:
200 g (7 oz) ricotta cheese
2 egg yolks, lightly beaten
75 g (3 oz) fontina cheese, finely grated
50 g (2 oz) black truffles, finely chopped
50 g (2 oz) black olives in oil, pitted and
    finely chopped
2 tablespoons chopped basil
1 tablespoon truffle oil
pinch of ground nutmeg
salt and pepper

To serve:
truffle shavings
truffle oil
rocket leaves
coarsely ground black pepper

Serves 4
Preparation time: 1 hour, plus relaxing
    the dough
Cooking time: 2 minutes

If you don't already have one, it's worth investing in a pasta machine for recipes such as this one, as rolling pasta by hand is laborious and time-consuming. Once you've tried making your own pasta, especially for ravioli and stuffed pasta, you won't want to buy the dried sort again.

1 To make the pasta, put the flour and a pinch of salt in a bowl. Make a well in the centre and break the eggs into the well. Stir them in a circular motion, gradually incorporating all the flour from the side of the bowl until you have a dough. Roll the dough into a ball, place it on a floured board and press flat. Use the heel of your hand to knead the dough firmly from the centre upwards then fold it in half and rotate the dough 90 degrees clockwise. Repeat this process, always turning the dough in the same direction, for at least 15 minutes until the dough is very smooth and elastic. Cover the dough loosely with clingfilm and leave it to relax for 1 hour.

2 Divide the dough into 3 pieces and cover them with a damp cloth. Take one piece of dough at a time, lightly dust it with flour and flatten it with your hand. Set the pasta machine to its widest setting, roll the dough through once, then put it on a work surface. Fold the dough by bringing the top third down and the bottom third up, then sprinkle it lightly with flour and roll it through the same setting again. Repeat 3 times on the same setting.

3 Start making the pasta thinner by working your way down the settings, only rolling it through once per setting this time, until you reach the second from lowest setting. Cover the rolled pasta with a damp cloth and repeat the whole process with the remaining pieces of dough.

4 Mix together all the filling ingredients and season with salt and pepper. Place small teaspoons of the filling on the pasta sheets, about 5 cm (2 inches) apart, moisten the edges of the dough and put a second sheet on top. Push down along the moistened edges so that each mound of filling is sealed well. Use a pastry cutter to cut the pasta into 5 cm (2 inch) squares.

5 Bring a large saucepan of water to a rolling boil. Add 1 tablespoon of salt and gently lift the ravioli into the pan. Cook for 2 minutes, then drain and serve immediately with truffle shavings, a drizzle of truffle oil, some rocket leaves and a dusting of fresh, coarsely ground black pepper.

stuffed vine leaves with yogurt and mint dip

100 ml (3½ fl oz) Greek olive oil

1 small onion, finely chopped

1 small red pepper, cored, deseeded
and chopped

2 garlic cloves, crushed

pinch of ground allspice

½ teaspoon ground cinnamon

125 g (4 oz) American long-grain rice,
rinsed in cold water

100 ml (3½ fl oz) white wine

200 ml (7 fl oz) water

grated rind and juice of 1 lemon

75 g (3 oz) pitted black Greek olives,
finely chopped

2 tablespoons pine nuts

75 g (3 oz) feta cheese, crumbled

4 tablespoons chopped parsley

1–2 tablespoons chopped dill

48 vine leaves, soaked in water

3 garlic cloves, sliced

salt and pepper

Yogurt and mint dip:
250 g (8 oz) natural yogurt

2 tablespoons chopped mint

2 small garlic cloves, sliced

½ cucumber, deseeded and coarsely
grated

Serves 4–6
Preparation time: 40 minutes,
plus cooling
Cooking time: about 2 hours

Dolmades, to give stuffed vine leaves their Greek name, are fiddly and time-consuming to make, but it is time well spent. Serve them as a starter alone or with other mezze dishes and a bottle of ice-cold retsina.

1 Heat 3 tablespoons of the olive oil in a large frying pan over a moderate heat and gently fry the onion and red pepper until soft. Increase the heat, add the garlic and cook for 1–2 minutes.

2 Add the allspice and cinnamon and fry for 1 minute, then stir in the rice and coat it thoroughly. Pour in the white wine and water, add the lemon rind and black olives and season well with salt and pepper. Bring the mixture to the boil, then reduce the heat and simmer gently for 15–20 minutes until the rice is cooked and the mixture is rich and thick. Set aside and leave to cool.

3 Heat a dry nonstick frying pan and toast the pine nuts over a moderately low heat, moving them quickly around the pan, until they are golden brown. When the rice mixture is cold, stir in the feta cheese, pine nuts and herbs and season to taste. Drain the vine leaves and arrange about 8 of them at the bottom of a heatproof casserole.

4 Put 1 of the remaining leaves, veined-side up, on a work surface and place 1 teaspoon of the mixture at the stalk end of the leaf. Bring the sides of the leaf over the filling, then roll up the leaf to form a firm but not too tight sausage shape. Place, seam-side down, in the casserole. Continue with the remaining leaves and olive mixture.

5 Squeeze lemon juice over the leaves, drizzle with the remaining olive oil and scatter with the slices of garlic. Place a snug-fitting heatproof plate directly on top of the vine leaves to stop them from unrolling while they are cooking, cover the casserole and cook in a preheated oven, 180°C (350°F), Gas Mark 4, for 1½ hours.

6 Meanwhile, mix together all the ingredients for the dip and transfer to a bowl. Divide the cooked stuffed vine leaves between plates, pour over the cooking juices and serve hot, tepid or cold with the yogurt and mint dip.

black bean patties with mango and chilli salsa

250 g (8 oz) dried black beans, soaked
    in water overnight
1 litre (1¾ pints) vegetable stock, plus
    extra if necessary
400 g (13 oz) can pinto beans
8 tablespoons olive oil
1 white onion, finely chopped
1 green pepper, finely chopped
5 cm (2 inch) cube fresh root ginger,
    peeled and grated
3 garlic cloves, chopped
2 teaspoons ground cumin
2 teaspoons ground coriander
1 teaspoon chilli powder
1 tablespoon tamarind paste
2 teaspoons dried oregano
small bunch of coriander, chopped
1 teaspoon hot pepper sauce
flour, for dusting
salt and pepper
green salad, to serve

Mango and chilli salsa:
4 tablespoons lime-flavoured olive oil
1 ripe but firm mango, peeled and diced
1 pink grapefruit, peeled and chopped
4 radishes, thinly sliced
2 tablespoons chopped coriander
1 red chilli, finely chopped
pinch of sugar
salt and pepper

Serves 4
Preparation time: 30 minutes,
    plus chilling
Cooking time: about 1½ hours

If you can't find lime-flavoured olive oil, use extra virgin olive oil flavoured with 1 teaspoon of finely grated lime rind instead.

1 Drain and rinse the black beans. Bring the stock to a boil in a large saucepan and cook the beans for 1 hour 10 minutes, adding more stock if necessary. Drain the beans, tip them into a food processor and add the pinto beans. Process briefly until the beans are broken down but not smooth, then transfer to a large bowl.

2 Heat 4 tablespoons of the olive oil in a large, heavy-based saucepan, add the onion, green pepper, ginger and garlic and cook gently for 12 minutes until softened. Stir in the cumin, coriander and chilli powder and fry for 2–3 minutes. Add to the bowl of beans with the tamarind paste, herbs and hot pepper sauce. Season with salt and pepper and mix well. Use your hands to form into 12 patties, then cover and chill in the refrigerator for 1 hour. Meanwhile, combine all the salsa ingredients in a dish and set aside until required.

3 Lightly dust the patties with flour. Heat the remaining olive oil in a large frying pan and gently fry the patties for 2–3 minutes, turning them once, until they are hot, golden and crispy. You may need to do this in 2–3 batches. Drain on kitchen paper and serve immediately with the mango and chilli salsa and a green salad.

spinach and sweet potato cakes with red chilli and coconut dip

500 g (1 lb) sweet potatoes, peeled and
    cut into chunks
125 g (4 oz) spinach leaves
4–5 spring onions, finely sliced
125 g (4 oz) mangetout, finely shredded
75 g (3 oz) sweetcorn
50 g (2 oz) pitted black olives, finely
    chopped
olive oil, for deep-frying
3 tablespoons sesame seeds
4 tablespoons flour
salt and pepper

Red chilli and coconut dip:
200 ml (7 fl oz) coconut cream
2 red chillies, deseeded and finely
    chopped
1 lemon grass stalk, thinly sliced
3 kaffir lime leaves, shredded
1 small bunch of coriander, chopped
    (including the stalks)
1 tablespoon light soy sauce
2 tablespoons sesame oil

To garnish:
lime wedges
spring onions, shredded

Serves 4
Preparation time: 35 minutes,
    plus infusing
Cooking time: about 40 minutes

Finely shredded mangetout, sweetcorn and chopped black olives add a variety of colours and flavours to these little sweet potato cakes, which are further enhanced by a spicy coconut dip.

1 Bring a large saucepan of salted water to the boil, add the sweet potatoes and cook for about 20 minutes until tender. Drain the potatoes, then return them to the pan and place over a low heat for 1 minute, stirring constantly to evaporate any excess moisture. Lightly mash the potatoes with a fork.

2 Meanwhile, put the spinach leaves in a colander and pour over a pan of boiling water. Rinse the spinach with cold water and squeeze the leaves dry. Stir the wilted spinach into the potatoes, then add the spring onions, mangetout, sweetcorn and olives. Season well with salt and pepper and set aside to cool.

3 To make the dip, gently warm the coconut cream in a small saucepan with the chillies, lemon grass and lime leaves for about 10 minutes, without letting it reach boiling point. Set aside to infuse.

4 Heat the oil in a large saucepan or deep-fat fryer to 180°C (350°F) or until a cube of bread browns in 20 seconds. Use your hands to form the potato mixture into 12 little cakes. Mix the sesame seeds and flour together and sprinkle the mixture over the cakes. Carefully lower the potato cakes into the hot oil with a slotted metal spoon and fry in batches for about 3 minutes until they are golden and crispy. Drain on kitchen paper and keep them warm while you cook the rest.

5 Stir the coriander, soy sauce and sesame oil into the dip and pour it into individual dishes. Serve immediately with the potato cakes, garnished with lime wedges and shredded spring onions.

gnocchi with gruyère and wild mushroom sauce

Wild mushroom sauce:
3 tablespoons olive oil
4 long shallots, finely chopped
25 g (1 oz) dried wild mushrooms,
    soaked in 200 ml (7 fl oz) boiling
    water according to packet
    instructions
1 tablespoon chopped lemon thyme,
    plus 4 sprigs for garnishing
200 ml (7 fl oz) double cream
1 tablespoon lemon juice
1 tablespoon roughly chopped parsley

Gnocchi:
1 kg (2 lb) floury potatoes, such as King
    Edwards, scrubbed
2 eggs
50 g (2 oz) stoned black Italian olives,
    chopped
4 sage leaves, shredded
½ teaspoon ground nutmeg
150 g (5 oz) plain flour
125 g (4 oz) aged Gruyère cheese,
    grated
pepper

Serves 4
Preparation time: 20 minutes
Cooking time: about 1¼ hours

Gnocchi are a speciality of northern Italy. The black olives in this recipe add an extra piquancy and combine well with the creamy wild mushroom sauce.

1 Heat the oil in a small frying pan and gently fry the shallots until soft and golden. Drain the mushrooms, reserving the soaking liquor, and thinly slice. Add to the shallots and cook for 1–2 minutes, then stir in the lemon thyme, cream, lemon juice, parsley and the mushroom soaking liquor. Simmer gently for 2 minutes, then set aside.

2 To make the gnocchi, put the potatoes in a baking tin and bake in a preheated oven, 190°C (375°F), Gas Mark 5, for about 50 minutes or until tender.

3 Carefully split open the baked potatoes and scrape the cooked flesh into a large bowl, mashing it lightly as you go. While the potato is still hot, quickly beat in the eggs, olives, sage, nutmeg, pepper to taste and enough flour to form a soft, sticky dough.

4 Use a spoon to take small amounts of the potato and roll them into oval balls. Arrange them side by side on a floured baking sheet and flatten slightly with the back of a fork to make the familiar gnocchi shape.

5 Bring a large pan of salted water to the boil, drop in about 10 gnocchi and cook for about 3–5 minutes or until they rise to the surface of the water. Lift them out with a slotted spoon and drain on kitchen paper. Cook the remaining gnocchi in batches, then arrange them in a buttered gratin dish large enough to take all the gnocchi in a single layer.

6 Pour the mushroom sauce over the gnocchi, mix gently and sprinkle with the grated Gruyère. Bake in a preheated oven, 240°C (475°F), Gas Mark 9, for 6–8 minutes until bubbling and golden. Serve garnished with lemon thyme.

fish and seafood

crab, coriander and lime briks with harissa

Harissa:

1½ tablespoons cumin seeds

2 teaspoons caraway seeds

1 tablespoon coriander seeds

25 g (1 oz) dried red chillies, soaked in
    boiling water for 3–4 hours

4 garlic cloves

100 g (3½ oz) roasted red peppers in
    olive oil, drained

1 teaspoon hot smoked paprika

1 tablespoon coarse sea salt

1 tablespoon aged sherry vinegar

100 ml (3½ fl oz) extra virgin olive oil

salt and pepper

Crab briks:

300 g (10 oz) cooked fresh or canned
    crab meat

finely grated rind of 2 limes

2 tablespoons lime juice

2 tablespoons chopped coriander

2 tablespoons chopped mint

½ teaspoon finely chopped chilli

1 teaspoon crushed garlic

75 g (3 oz) chilli-stuffed green olives,
    roughly chopped

½ teaspoon ground coriander

salt and pepper

8 sheets of filo pastry

mild olive oil, for deep-frying

Serves 4

Preparation time: 40 minutes,
    plus soaking

Cooking time: 6–10 minutes

Real brik pastry, or warka *to use its Tunisian name, can be difficult to find, but filo pastry works just as well. Serve these crab briks with a crisp green salad.*

1 First make the harissa. Put the cumin, caraway and coriander seeds in a heavy-based frying pan and dry-roast over a moderate heat until they begin to give off an aromatic smell. Tip the seeds into a mortar and grind to a coarse mixture.

2 Drain the chillies, discarding the soaking liquor. Roughly chop them and place in a food processor with the garlic, roasted peppers, paprika and sea salt. Blend until completely smooth, then transfer to a bowl. Stir in the sherry vinegar and toasted spices then the olive oil. Season to taste with salt and pepper. Cover and chill in the refrigerator until required.

3 To make the briks, put the crab in a large bowl, discarding any bits of shell or cartilage. Add the lime rind and juice, coriander, mint, chilli, garlic, green olives and ground coriander, season with salt and pepper and mix well. Spread out a double layer of filo pastry and place a quarter of the crab mixture in the centre of each one. Wrap into a parcel, moistening the edges so that they stick together and seal the filling.

4 Heat the olive oil in a large saucepan or wok to 180°C (350°F) until a cube of bread browns in 20 seconds. Gently lower the briks into the oil and deep-fry for 2–3 minutes until golden brown and crispy. You will need to do this in 2–3 batches. Drain on kitchen paper and serve immediately with salad leaves and the harissa.

skate wings with caper and olive butter

4 tablespoons extra virgin olive oil

4 skate wings, about 250 g (8 oz) each, trimmed

4 tablespoons flour, seasoned with salt and pepper

herb and baby leaf salad, to serve

Caper and olive butter:

100 g (3½ oz) butter

1 garlic clove, chopped

2 tablespoons capers in brine, drained

50 g (2 oz) pitted black olives

juice of 1 lemon

1 tablespoon chopped curly parsley

1 tablespoon chopped chervil

salt and pepper

Serves 4

Preparation time: 10 minutes

Cooking time: about 10 minutes

This unusual butter flavoured with capers and black olives combined with lemon juice, garlic and herbs makes a lively accompaniment to pan-fried skate. It is essential that this dish is prepared quickly and served immediately.

1 Heat the oil in a large frying pan over a moderately high heat. Sprinkle the skate wings with a little seasoned flour and place in the pan. You may need to do this in 2 batches. Fry the skate for about 2–3 minutes on each side until cooked through, then place on hot serving plates.

2 To make the caper and olive butter, wipe the pan with kitchen paper and return it to the heat. Melt the butter and when the frothiness has died down add the garlic and bubble gently until it turns golden brown. Tip in the capers, olives, lemon juice, parsley and chervil and stir quickly for 20 seconds. Season with salt and pepper and pour a little of the butter over each skate wing. Serve immediately with a herb and baby leaf salad.

roasted cod with olive and thyme polenta

5–6 thyme sprigs

4 chunky cod fillets, about 200 g (7 oz)
  each

6 tablespoons extra virgin olive oil,
  plus extra for drizzling

3–4 spring onions, finely sliced

450 ml (¾ pint) boiling water

200 g (7 oz) polenta flour

2 teaspoons chopped thyme

100 g (3½ oz) pitted black olives

75 g (3 oz) freshly grated Parmesan
  cheese

salt and pepper

Serves 4
Preparation time: 8 minutes
Cooking time: 15–20 minutes

1 Put the thyme sprigs in a roasting tin, then add the cod fillets, skin-side down, so that each one is on a thyme sprig. Drizzle with 2 tablespoons of the olive oil and season well with salt and pepper. Cook in a preheated oven, 190°C (375°F), Gas Mark 5, for 15–20 minutes or until the fillets are cooked through.

2 Meanwhile, heat 2 more tablespoons of the oil in a large saucepan and gently fry the spring onions for 1–2 minutes until soft. Pour the boiling water into the pan and add the polenta flour in a steady stream, stirring constantly. Reduce the heat and let the polenta bubble gently for about 5 minutes until cooked, stirring constantly. Add the thyme, olives, Parmesan and the remaining oil, stir well and season to taste with salt and pepper.

3 Divide the polenta among 4 warm plates, top with a piece of roasted cod and an extra drizzle of olive oil and serve immediately.

pan-fried wild salmon with porcini on horseradish-spiked mash

1 kg (2 lb) floury potatoes, cut into large
    chunks
100 ml (3½ fl oz) extra virgin olive oil
4 wild salmon fillets, about 175 g
    (6 oz) each
125 g (4 oz) porcini mushrooms, thickly
    sliced
2 garlic cloves, chopped
2 tablespoons roughly chopped parsley
2 tablespoons creamed horseradish
salt and pepper
snipped chives, to garnish

Serves 4
Preparation time: 10 minutes
Cooking time: 25 minutes

In this recipe, the potatoes are mashed with olive oil, which gives a wonderfully rich and surprisingly creamy result.

1 Bring a large saucepan of salted water to the boil and drop in the potatoes. Cook for 20 minutes or until soft.

2 Meanwhile, heat 2 tablespoons of the olive oil in a frying pan over a moderately high heat and put the salmon fillets, skin-side down, into the pan. Fry the fillets for 2–3 minutes, then turn them over and cook for another 1–2 minutes until they are almost cooked through. Remove the fillets from the pan and keep them warm.

3 Wipe the pan with kitchen paper and add 2 more tablespoons of the oil. Place the pan over a moderate heat, add the sliced mushrooms and cook for 3–4 minutes until golden and soft. Add the chopped garlic and cook for 1–2 minutes, then turn off the heat.

4 Drain the potatoes and return them to the pan, put it over a low heat and stir the potatoes for just 1 minute, to evaporate any excess water and dry them a little. Using a potato masher or a potato ricer, mash the potatoes until they are smooth and lump-free. Stir in the remaining olive oil, parsley and creamed horseradish and season to taste with salt and pepper.

5 Dollop the potatoes on to warm plates, put the salmon on top and scatter with the mushrooms. Garnish with chives and serve immediately.

griddled tuna steaks with white bean salad

5 tablespoons extra virgin olive oil, plus extra for drizzling

grated rind and juice of 1 lemon

1 garlic clove, crushed

400 g (13 oz) can cannellini beans

1 red onion, finely chopped

75 g (3 oz) pitted black dry-cured olives, halved

small bunch of flat leaf parsley, roughly chopped

4 tuna steaks, about 175 g (6 oz) each

1 teaspoon mixed peppercorns, freshly crushed

salt

lemon wedges, to serve

Serves 4
Preparation time: 10 minutes
Cooking time: 3–4 minutes

This quick recipe is a good example of the Mediterranean diet, combining oily fish, pulses and, of course, liberal quantities of olives and olive oil.

1 Whisk 3 tablespoons of the olive oil, the lemon rind and juice and crushed garlic in a bowl. Season well with salt and pepper.

2 Drain and rinse the cannellini beans, put them in a large bowl with the chopped onion, olives and parsley and stir to combine. Pour the dressing over the beans and set them aside for the flavour to develop while you prepare the fish.

3 Rub the tuna steaks with the remaining olive oil and season with a little salt and the crushed mixed peppercorns. Heat a griddle pan until hot and cook the tuna steaks for 3–4 minutes, turning them once, until cooked and nicely seared, but still a little rare. Set aside to rest for 1–2 minutes.

4 Divide the bean salad among 4 serving plates. Top the beans with the tuna steaks, drizzle with olive oil and serve with lemon wedges.

curried monkfish with mushroom and olive pilau

4 tablespoons olive oil

1 teaspoon mustard seeds

1 large onion, sliced

2 teaspoons grated fresh root ginger

4 garlic cloves, sliced

1 teaspoon ground turmeric

½ teaspoon chilli powder

½ teaspoon ground cinnamon

1 tablespoon ground coriander

1 teaspoon ground cumin

3 fresh tomatoes, skinned, deseeded
    and roughly chopped

1 tablespoon dark brown sugar

200 ml (7 fl oz) coconut milk

pinch of saffron threads

150 ml (¼ pint) water

500 g (1 lb) monkfish fillet, cubed

4 tablespoons chopped coriander
    leaves, plus sprigs for garnishing

salt and pepper

crispy fried shallots, to garnish

Mushroom and olive pilau:

2 tablespoons olive oil

4 cardamom pods

2 cloves

200 g (7 oz) button mushrooms, roughly
    chopped

65 g (2½ oz) pitted black olives, chopped

300 g (10 oz) basmati rice

½ teaspoon salt

500 ml (17 fl oz) boiling water

Serves 4

Preparation time: 20 minutes

Cooking time: 40–50 minutes

1 Heat 1 tablespoon of the olive oil in a small frying pan and fry the mustard seeds until they begin to pop. Set aside.

2 Heat the remaining oil in a large, deep frying pan over a moderate heat and fry the onion for 4–5 minutes until soft and browned at the edges. Add the ginger and garlic and fry for a further 2 minutes. Add the spices and cook for 1–2 minutes, stirring constantly. Add the tomatoes, sugar, coconut milk, saffron and fried mustard seeds. Pour in the water, season well with salt and pepper and bring the mixture to simmering point. Leave over a low heat for about 15 minutes.

3 Meanwhile, cook the pilau. Heat the olive oil in a large saucepan, add the cardamom, cloves and mushrooms and fry gently until the mushrooms are soft and golden and the spices release an aromatic smell. Add the chopped olives, rice, salt and the measurement water and bring to the boil. Reduce the heat, cover the pan and leave to simmer gently for 10–12 minutes until the rice is cooked.

4 Stir the monkfish into the curry sauce and simmer gently for 7–8 minutes or until cooked. Stir in the chopped coriander. Serve the monkfish with the fluffy pilau rice and sprinkled with crispy fried challots and coriander sprigs.

whole snapper with roasted mediterranean vegetables

Roasted Mediterranean vegetables:
1 fennel head, cut into wedges
2 red peppers, cored, deseeded and cut
    into large chunks
6–7 garlic cloves, unpeeled
1 aubergine, sliced lengthways
2 courgettes, sliced lengthways
2 tablespoons basil oil
2 tablespoons extra virgin olive oil
sea salt and pepper

4 whole red snappers, about 250 g
    (8 oz) each
grated rind of 1 lemon, plus extra for
    serving
3 tablespoons Spanish extra virgin
    olive oil
2 garlic cloves, chopped
1 tablespoon chopped fennel fronds
    or dill
100 g (3½ oz) large green olives, plus
    extra for serving
200 g (7 oz) green beans, topped and
    tailed
lemon wedges, to serve

Serves 4
Preparation time: 10 minutes
Cooking time: about 50 minutes

This recipe also works fantastically well with mullet or bream. The olives will add flavour and moisture to the fish as it cooks.

1 To prepare the roasted vegetables, put the fennel, red peppers, garlic, aubergine and courgettes in a large roasting tin and toss with the basil oil and olive oil. Scatter with sea salt and pepper to taste and roast in a preheated oven, 190°C (375°F), Gas Mark 5, for about 50 minutes until the vegetables are cooked and slightly charred.

2 Meanwhile, slash the skin of the snappers and rub them all over with the lemon rind, olive oil, garlic and fennel fronds or dill. Arrange the fish side by side in a roasting tin so that they fit in snugly, scatter over the olives and bake in the oven with the vegetables for about 20 minutes until the fish are cooked through and the skins are golden and crispy.

3 Bring a pan of salted water to the boil and cook the green beans for about 4 minutes until al dente. When the roasted vegetables are ready, toss them with the cooked green beans.

4 Serve each snapper scattered with a few strands of lemon rind, some extra green olives, a lemon wedge and the roasted vegetables and beans.

balsamic-glazed swordfish with asparagus

100 ml (3½ fl oz) aged reduced balsamic
  vinegar
5 tablespoons extra virgin olive oil
1 tablespoon Harissa (see page 48)
2 tablespoons green olive paste
4 thick swordfish steaks, about 200 g
  (7 oz) each
75 g (3 oz) small black Tuscan olives
300 g (10 oz) asparagus spears
salt and pepper

Serves 4
Preparation time: 8 minutes,
  plus marinating
Cooking time: about 25 minutes

1 Mix together the balsamic vinegar, 3 tablespoons of the olive oil, the harissa and green olive paste and place in a bowl. Add the swordfish steaks and leave to marinate for about 1 hour.

2 Remove the fish from the marinade, pat dry with kitchen paper and set aside. Pour the marinade into a small saucepan and heat gently until bubbling. Leave to simmer for 2–3 minutes then remove from the heat.

3 Put the olives and remaining olive oil in a bowl, add the asparagus spears and toss well. Season generously with salt and pepper and tip into a roasting tin. Bake in a preheated oven, 190°C (375°F), Gas Mark 5, for about 12 minutes until the asparagus is cooked and golden.

4 Heat a frying pan until hot and cook the swordfish steaks for 6–8 minutes, turning them once, until they are almost cooked through.

5 Arrange the asparagus spears and olives on warm serving plates, top with the swordfish steaks and drizzle over the balsamic glaze. Serve immediately.

moules à la provençale

It is very important when cooking mussels that they are scrupulously clean before you start to cook, so scrub them thoroughly under cold running water and throw away any damaged ones or any that won't close when you tap them.

1 Heat 3 tablespoons of the olive oil in a large, deep frying pan or flameproof casserole, add the chopped shallots and cook over a moderate heat for 3 minutes until they are soft and lightly golden. Add the garlic and fry for 2 minutes. Stir in the plum tomatoes, thyme, rosemary, olives and white wine, then cover the pan and leave to simmer gently for about 20 minutes.

2 Meanwhile, scrub and clean the mussels thoroughly, removing any beards, and discard any damaged ones, or ones that will not close when tapped sharply.

3 Tip the mussels into the pan of sauce, add the remaining olive oil and stir to coat them thoroughly. Cover with a lid and cook for 4–5 minutes until all the mussels have opened (discard any that have not).

4 Heap the mussels into deep bowls, garnish with torn basil leaves and serve with lots of crusty bread.

6 tablespoons French extra virgin
   olive oil
4 shallots, chopped
3 garlic cloves, chopped
400 g (13 oz) can plum tomatoes
2 thyme sprigs, leaves removed and
   chopped
1 rosemary sprig, leaves removed and
   chopped
100 g (3½ oz) cured black olives in oil,
   drained
150 ml (¼ pint) dry white wine
1.75 kg (3½ lb) mussels
torn basil leaves, to garnish
crusty bread, to serve

Serves 4
Preparation time: 12 minutes
Cooking time: 30 minutes

pan-fried scallops and spicy salsa with olive and parmesan crisps

Salsa:
6 tablespoons extra virgin olive oil
2–3 tablespoons lemon juice
6 cherry tomatoes, quartered
25 g (1 oz) pitted black olives, quartered
3 anchovies in olive oil, drained and
    chopped (optional)
1 tablespoon chopped dill
2 spring onions, finely sliced

Olive and Parmesan crisps:
65 g (2½ oz) finely grated Parmesan
    cheese
65 g (2½ oz) pitted black olives,
    chopped

20–24 scallops, corals removed
3 tablespoons extra virgin olive oil
finely grated rind of 1 lemon
2 teaspoons fennel seeds
salt and pepper
frisée lettuce, to serve

Serves 4
Preparation time: 15 minutes
Cooking time: 8 minutes

If you find your olives too salty, put them in a pan of cold water, bring it to the boil and simmer for 2 minutes, then drain and rinse thoroughly with cold water before using them in recipes.

1 Combine all the salsa ingredients in a small bowl and set aside. To make the Parmesan crisps, mix together the grated Parmesan and the chopped olives, then make 12 little flat rounds of the mixture on 2 nonstick baking trays, leaving room for them to spread. Bake them in a preheated oven, 180°C (350°F), Gas Mark 4, for 4–5 minutes until they are crisp and golden. Leave to cool slightly, then carefully lift them on to a wire rack with a palette knife to cool completely.

2 Toss the scallops in 1 tablespoon of the olive oil with the lemon rind and fennel seeds and season with salt and pepper. Heat the remaining oil on a flat griddle over a moderately high heat and place the scallops on the pan, cook for about 1 minute, then turn them over and cook for 1 minute on the other side.

3 Remove the scallops with tongs, arrange them on warm serving plates and drizzle with the salsa. Serve immediately with the crisps and some frisée lettuce.

hot and sour tamarind fishcakes with sweet shallot and chive dipping sauce

Hot and sour tamarind fishcakes:
200 g (7 oz) cod fillet, cut into chunks
150 g (5 oz) salmon fillet, cut into chunks
150 g (5 oz) raw peeled prawns, cut into
    chunks
2 tablespoons Thai red curry paste
1 tablespoon tamarind paste
2 teaspoons palm or dark muscovado
    sugar
2 tablespoons Thai fish sauce
75 g (3 oz) green beans, very thinly sliced
1 kaffir lime leaf, very finely sliced
2 garlic cloves, chopped
1 lemon grass stalk, finely chopped
2 tablespoons Lemon Grass, Ginger and
    Lime Leaf Oil (see page 19)
1 small egg, lightly beaten
1–2 tablespoons rice flour
olive oil, for shallow frying
lime wedges, to serve

Sweet shallot and chive dipping sauce:
3 shallots, finely chopped
2 tablespoons palm or muscovado sugar
1 red chilli, thinly sliced
2 tablespoons Thai fish sauce
100 ml (3½ fl oz) rice vinegar
2 tablespoons Lemon Grass, Ginger and
    Lime Leaf Oil (see page 19)
2 tablespoons snipped Chinese chives

Serves 4
Preparation time: 40 minutes
Cooking time: about 25 minutes

The Asian flavours here work fantastically well with fish. Make sure the oil is nice and hot before you start frying so the fishcakes don't soak up too much of the oil.

1   Put all the fishcake ingredients except the rice flour into a food processor and blend several times until you have a rough but well-mixed paste. Scrape into a large bowl and work in the flour. The mixture should not be too stiff but thick enough to form into cakes.

2   With damp hands, form the mixture into about 20 small balls and flatten them slightly. Put them in the refrigerator while you make the sauce.

3   To make the dipping sauce, combine all the ingredients except the chives in a small pan and set over a very low heat for about 10 minutes for the flavours to develop and the sugar to dissolve. Add the chives to the sauce just before serving.

4   Heat enough olive oil in a wok or large frying pan to shallow fry the fishcakes. Fry them in batches for 3–4 minutes each, turning them once, until they are cooked and golden. Drain on kitchen paper and serve immediately with the dipping sauce and some lime wedges.

tandoori prawns with carrot and mustard salad

750 g (1½ lb) raw tiger prawns, peeled
2 tablespoons Cumin, Coriander and
   Cardamom Oil (see page 19)

Marinade:
125 g (4 oz) full-fat natural yogurt
2.5 cm (1 inch) cube fresh root ginger,
   peeled and grated
1 large garlic clove, crushed
1 teaspoon ground coriander
½ teaspoon ground turmeric
3 teaspoons ground hot tandoori mix
1 tablespoon lemon juice
salt and pepper

Carrot and mustard seed salad:
1 tablespoon extra virgin olive oil
2 teaspoons mustard seeds
4 carrots, grated
2 tablespoons Cumin, Coriander and
   Cardamom Oil (see page 19)
2 tablespoons lemon juice
pinch of sugar
3 tablespoons roughly chopped parsley
2 shallots, finely chopped
50 g (2 oz) pitted black olives, chopped

To serve:
deep-fried poppadums
Indian pickles

Serves 4
Preparation time: 30 minutes,
   plus marinating
Cooking time: 20–22 minutes

1 Mix together all the marinade ingredients in a bowl and season with salt and pepper. Stir in the prawns until they are thoroughly covered. Cover and set aside in the refrigerator for about 6 hours.

2 Tip the prawns into a roasting tin and bake in a preheated oven, 200°C (400°F), Gas Mark 6, for 18–20 minutes until they are cooked.

3 To make the salad, heat the oil in a small, heavy frying pan and fry the mustard seeds and heat for 1–2 minutes or until they begin to pop. Mix the mustard seeds with the remaining salad ingredients and set aside until required.

4 Arrange the prawns in individual serving dishes and drizzle with the cumin, coriander and cardamom oil.

5 Put the salad in a serving bowl and serve with the tandoori-style prawns, some crisp poppadums and mixed Indian pickles.

buttery lobster tails with aïoli

Aïoli:
1 large egg yolk
3–4 garlic cloves, crushed
1 tablespoon lemon juice
175 ml (6 fl oz) extra virgin olive oil
1 tablespoon snipped chives
salt and pepper

4 raw lobster tails
50 g (2 oz) butter
2 tablespoons Garlic and Saffron Oil
    (see page 19)
finely grated rind of 1 lemon
2 tablespoons chopped chervil, plus
    extra sprigs, for garnishing
cucumber ribbons, made using a
    vegetable peeler, to serve

Serves 4
Preparation time: 20 minutes
Cooking time: 7–8 minutes

Always make sure that all your ingredients are at room temperature to ensure that you produce a successful aïoli.

1 To make the aïoli, beat the egg yolk in a bowl with the garlic, lemon juice and a large pinch of salt and pepper, either by hand or with an electric whisk. Gradually add the olive oil, drop by drop, beating constantly until it is all completely incorporated and you have a thick, smooth emulsion. Stir in the chives and season to taste with salt and pepper.

2 Dot the lobster tails with the butter and drizzle with the garlic and saffron oil. Place the lobster tails, flesh-side up, under a preheated grill for 7–8 minutes until cooked through. Sprinkle with the lemon rind and chopped chervil and serve immediately with the cucumber ribbons and home-made aïoli in small bowls.

meat
and poultry

slow-cooked beef and olive casserole

1 kg (2 lb) shin of beef, or stewing
    steak, cubed
3 tablespoons extra virgin olive oil
200 g (7 oz) streaky bacon, chopped
20 baby onions
200 g (7 oz) carrots, cut into chunks
375 g (12 oz) celeriac, cut into chunks
6 garlic cloves
2 tablespoons plain flour
450 ml (¾ pint) beef stock
100 g (3½ oz) black olives
2 thick strips of orange peel
200 g (7 oz) large field mushrooms,
    halved
1 rosemary sprig
2–3 thyme sprigs
chopped parsley, to garnish
mashed potato, to serve

Marinade:
1 large onion, roughly chopped
750 ml (1¼ pints) white wine
2 tablespoons extra virgin olive oil
2 garlic cloves, roughly chopped
2 bay leaves
1 small bunch of parsley
2–3 thyme sprigs
1 rosemary sprig
2 tablespoons brandy
8 black peppercorns

Serves 4–6
Preparation time: 30 minutes,
    plus marinating
Cooking time: 3½–4 hours

Black olives and orange peel are traditional flavourings in the slow-cooked beef daubes of Provence. Using white wine instead of the more familiar red gives this casserole an attractively light flavour.

1 Put the cubed beef and all the marinade ingredients in a large bowl. Cover and leave to marinate in the refrigerator for 24 hours.

2 Strain the meat and pat dry on kitchen paper, reserving the marinade liquor. Heat the olive oil in a large, flameproof casserole and fry the beef in batches to seal. Lift out the beef with a slotted spoon and set aside. Quickly fry the bacon, then lift it out and add to the beef. Tip the onions into the casserole and fry until they are soft and golden. Remove them and brown the carrots, celeriac and garlic, adding a little extra oil if necessary. Remove with a slotted spoon.

3 Stir the flour into the juices in the casserole and cook for 1 minute, then return the meat and its juices and the browned vegetables. Pour in the reserved marinade, beef stock, olives, orange peel, mushrooms, rosemary and thyme and bring up to a simmer.

4 Cover the casserole with a tight-fitting lid, place in a preheated oven, 140°C (275°F), Gas Mark 1, and cook very gently for 3–3½ hours until the meat is really tender.

5 Remove the casserole from the oven, sprinkle with chopped parsley and serve with creamy mashed potato.

bloody mary burgers with olive and onion jam

400 g (13 oz) minced rump or sirloin
   steak
150 g (5 oz) minced belly pork
5–6 tablespoons olive oil
3–4 shallots, chopped
1 large garlic clove, crushed
75 g (3 oz) chestnut mushrooms
1 tablespoon finely chopped
   cornichons or gherkins
2 tablespoons sun-dried tomato paste
1 teaspoon Dijon mustard
2 teaspoons Worcestershire sauce
1 teaspoon Tabasco sauce
1 tablespoon vodka
1 teaspoon celery salt
25 g (1 oz) panko crumbs
salt and pepper

Olive and onion jam:
3 tablespoons extra virgin olive oil
2 large red onions, thinly sliced
75 g (3 oz) pitted black olives in oil,
   drained
¼ teaspoon sugar
1 teaspoon chopped thyme
2 tablespoons sherry vinegar
2–3 tablespoons hot water

To serve:
toasted ciabatta rolls
celery sticks

Serves 4
Preparation time: 30 minutes,
   plus marinating
Cooking time: about 50 minutes

All the makings of a traditional Bloody Mary go into these burgers to make them into something special. If Japanese panko crumbs are unavailable, use coarse breadcrumbs instead.

1 Mix together the minced beef and pork in a large bowl and set aside. Heat 2–3 tablespoons of the olive oil in a frying pan over a moderate heat and fry the shallots and garlic until softened and golden. Stir in the mushrooms and cook for about 3 minutes until they are soft and cooked. Remove the mixture from the heat and allow to cool a little.

2 Add the cooled mushroom mixture to the meat with the remaining burger ingredients. Season well with salt and pepper and mix together really well with your hands until thoroughly combined. Using wet hands, form into 4 large burgers. Cover loosely with clingfilm and chill in the refrigerator until required.

3 To make the olive and onion jam, gently heat the olive oil in a heavy-based frying pan and stir in the onions. Fry over a very low heat for about 12–15 minutes until soft but not coloured. Stir in the olives, a pinch of salt, the sugar and thyme and pour in the sherry vinegar and hot water. Continue cooking very gently for 15–20 minutes until the onions and olives are soft and caramelized and no excess liquid remains. Allow to cool.

4 Heat the remaining 3 tablespoons of oil in a large frying pan, add the burgers and cook for about 3–4 minutes on each side. If you prefer your meat well done or rare, just add or subtract a minute on each side.

5 Serve the burgers on toasted ciabatta rolls with a dollop of the olive and onion jam and a celery stick.

fillet steak with mustard, tarragon, and olive tapanade

50 g (2 oz) butter

4 shallots, finely chopped

1 tablespoon wholegrain mustard

1 teaspoon Dijon mustard

2 tablespoons black olive tapenade paste

150 ml (¼ pint) cider

4 thick fillet steaks, about 200 g (7 oz) each, at room temperature

2 tablespoons coarsely ground black peppercorns

2 tablespoons extra virgin olive oil

2 tablespoons Calvados or brandy

2 tablespoons crème fraîche

2 tablespoons chopped tarragon

salt and pepper

To serve:

steamed asparagus

home-made chips

mustardy mayonnaise

Serves 4

Preparation time: 8 minutes

Cooking time: 14–16 minutes

1 Heat the butter in a frying pan until it has melted and is beginning to froth. Add the shallots and fry gently for 5–6 minutes until softened. Add the wholegrain and Dijon mustards and the tapenade paste and pour in the cider. Simmer gently for 2 minutes and remove from the heat.

2 Press the fillet steaks into the black pepper. Heat the olive oil in a large frying pan and cook the fillet steaks for 1–2 minutes on each side or longer if you like your meat well done. Pour over the Calvados or brandy and carefully set it alight.

3 Arrange the steaks on warm serving plates while you quickly scrape the Calvados and meat juices into the cider sauce. Stir in the crème fraîche and tarragon, season to taste with salt and pepper and gently warm the sauce without letting it boil. Pour a little sauce over each fillet steak and serve immediately with steamed asparagus, home-made chips and a dish of mustardy mayonnaise.

cumin and mint meatballs with rich tomato sauce and bulgar wheat

4–5 tablespoons extra virgin olive oil

1 onion, finely chopped

2 garlic cloves, crushed

1–2 teaspoons ground cumin

2 tablespoons pine nuts

475 g (15 oz) minced lamb

2 tablespoons chopped mint

2 tablespoons chopped parsley

1 teaspoon dried oregano

grated rind of ½ lemon

1 tablespoon clear honey

200 g (7 oz) bulgar wheat

salt and pepper

shredded mint leaves, to garnish

Tomato sauce:

2 teaspoons cumin seeds

6 tablespoons extra virgin olive oil

1 large onion, finely chopped

2 large garlic cloves, finely chopped

2 x 400 g (13 oz) cans chopped
    tomatoes

few strands of lemon rind

½ teaspoon sugar

½ teaspoon dried mint

300 ml (½ pint) cold water

400 ml (14 fl oz) hot water

Serves 4
Preparation time: 35 minutes
Cooking time: about 1¼ hours

1 Heat 2–3 tablespoons of the olive oil in a large frying pan and gently fry the onion and garlic for 3–4 minutes until soft and golden. Stir in the ground cumin and cook gently for 1–2 minutes. Meanwhile, heat a dry, nonstick frying pan and toast the pine nuts, moving them quickly around the pan until they are golden.

2 Remove the onion mixture from the pan and put it in a large bowl with the minced lamb, pine nuts, herbs, lemon rind and honey. Season with salt and pepper and mix together really well with your hands until thoroughly combined.

3 Using wet hands, form the lamb mixture into balls the size of golf balls – you should be able to make about 24. Cover and set aside while you make the tomato sauce.

4 Heat a small, dry frying pan over the heat and toast the cumin seeds until they give off an aromatic smell. Remove the pan from the heat.

5 Heat 3 tablespoons of the olive oil in a saucepan and fry the onion and garlic until soft but not coloured. Pour in the tomatoes and stir in the toasted cumin seeds, lemon rind, sugar and dried mint and season with salt and pepper. Pour in the cold water and leave the sauce to simmer gently over a very low heat for about 45 minutes until it is thick and glossy. Remove the pan from the heat and stir in the remaining olive oil.

6 Pour half the sauce into another saucepan with the hot water and stir in the bulgar wheat. Place the pan over the heat and bring to the boil, then reduce the heat and leave the bulgar wheat to cook very gently for about 12 minutes, adding a little more water if necessary. The bulgar wheat should absorb all the liquid and be dry and fluffy.

7 Meanwhile, heat the remaining 2 tablespoons of oil in a large frying pan and add the meatballs. Fry gently for about 10 minutes, turning them regularly so they are cooked and golden all over. Serve the meatballs with the tomato sauce and bulgar wheat, sprinkled with mint.

home-roast ham with black olive glaze

2 kg (4 lb) boned and rolled joint
   unsmoked gammon, soaked for
   12 hours or overnight
2 litres (3½ pints) dry cider
5–6 juniper berries
1 large onion, halved and sliced
1 fresh bay leaf
4–5 peppercorns
2 tablespoons black treacle
2 tablespoons black olive tapenade
2 tablespoons olive oil
2 teaspoons mustard powder
1 tablespoon Calvados
1 teaspoon mustard seeds
2 tablespoons dark brown sugar

To serve:
potato tortilla
crisp green salad

Serves 4–6
Preparation time: 20 minutes
Cooking time: 2¾ hours

1 Drain and rinse the gammon joint, then put it in a large, flameproof casserole. Pour in the cider and add the juniper berries, onion, bay leaf and peppercorns. Place the casserole over a moderate heat, bring it to the boil, then reduce the heat, part-cover the pan and simmer very gently for 2 hours.

2 Leave the ham to cool in the cooking liquor. When it is cool enough to handle easily, lift it out of the casserole and carefully cut off the skin with a sharp knife, making sure that you leave an even layer of fat on the ham. Use the same knife to score a criss-cross pattern in the fat – just deep enough to cut the fat but not so deep as to cut into the meat itself.

3 Mix together the treacle, tapenade, olive oil, mustard powder, Calvados, mustard seeds and sugar and spread the mixture evenly over the surface of the ham. Put the ham into a roasting tin and roast in a preheated oven, 200°C (400°F), Gas Mark 6, for 45 minutes until it is golden brown and bubbling, basting frequently.

4 Carve the ham into thin slices and serve immediately with a potato tortilla and a crisp green salad.

olivey lamb chops with lemon, caper and rocket couscous

6 anchovies in olive oil, drained and
  chopped
2 tablespoons black olive tapenade
  paste
2–3 thyme sprigs, leaves stripped and
  chopped
1 rosemary sprig, leaves stripped and
  chopped
2 bay leaves, torn
2–3 garlic cloves, crushed
finely grated rind of 1 lemon
4 tablespoons white wine
8 tablespoons extra virgin olive oil
8 lamb loin chops, about 150 g (5 oz)
  each
300 g (10 oz) medium-grain couscous
400 ml (14 fl oz) boiling water
2 tablespoons salted capers or capers
  in brine, rinsed and drained
100 g (3½ oz) spicy-marinated green
  olives, chopped
75 g (3 oz) wild rocket leaves, plus extra
  for serving
juice of 1 lemon, plus extra for serving
salt and pepper
lemon wedges, to serve

Serves 4
Preparation time: 25 minutes,
  plus marinating
Cooking time: 10–12 minutes

The combination of lamb, couscous and olives gives this dish a Moroccan feel. Lamb absorbs flavours well and this marinade will help to keep the meat tender while it is cooking.

1 Mash the anchovy fillets with a fork and stir them into a bowl with the tapenade paste. Add the herbs, garlic and lemon rind, then pour in the wine and 4 tablespoons of the olive oil. Stir thoroughly, then rub the mixture really well into the lamb chops. Cover and leave at room temperature for about 1 hour.

2 Put the couscous into a heatproof bowl and stir in 2 tablespoons of the remaining olive oil so that all the grains are covered. Season with salt and pour over the boiling water. Leave to stand for 5–8 minutes until the grains feel soft.

3 Heat a griddle pan until hot. Grind some black pepper over the chops and cook them for about 2 minutes. Sprinkle with a little salt, then cook the other side for a further 2 minutes. Transfer to a warm dish, cover with foil and leave to rest for 5 minutes.

4 Fluff up the couscous with a fork and gently fold in the capers, chopped olives and rocket and squeeze over the lemon juice. Heap the couscous on to warm plates and arrange a lamb chop on each one with a spoonful of its juices. Sprinkle with rocket leaves, drizzle with the remaining olive oil and an extra squeeze of lemon juice and serve immediately with lemon wedges.

sweet lamb tagine with new potatoes, lemons and olives

pinch of ground cloves
1 teaspoon ground turmeric
pinch of ground mace
1 teaspoon ground ginger
1 teaspoon ground coriander
1 teaspoon ground cumin
pinch of saffron threads
750 g (1½ lb) boned neck of lamb, cubed
300 g (10 oz) new potatoes, halved
12 ready-to-eat dried apricots
50 g (2 oz) raisins
2 tablespoons olive oil
1 large onion, sliced
2 garlic cloves, roughly chopped
5 cm (2 inch) cube fresh root ginger,
    peeled and grated
4 tablespoons clear Moroccan honey
4 tablespoons orange juice
3 tablespoons lemon juice
600 ml (1 pint) lamb stock
1 cinnamon stick
150 g (5 oz) green olives, cracked
    (see page 32)
1 preserved lemon, sliced
salt and pepper
lemon wedges, to serve

Serves 4
Preparation time: 25 minutes,
    plus marinating and standing
Cooking time: 1¾ hours

Preserved lemons are traditionally added to North African chicken tagines, but they also work very well here with the tender sweetness of lamb.

1 Put all the ground spices and the saffron in a heavy frying pan over a low heat and dry-fry gently for 1–2 minutes, stirring frequently. Remove the pan from the heat and leave the spices to cool. Rub the spice mixture generously into the lamb cubes. Cover and leave at room temperature for about 1 hour.

2 Arrange the potatoes in a tagine or casserole and add the marinated lamb, apricots and raisins.

3 Heat the olive oil in a frying pan and fry the onions for 3–4 minutes, then add the garlic and ginger. Fry for 1–2 minutes until lightly coloured, then tip the mixture over the lamb.

4 Pour the honey, orange juice and lemon juice into the tagine and add enough of the stock just to cover the lamb. Season well with salt and pepper, add the cinnamon stick, cracked green olives and preserved lemon and bring up to boiling point over a moderate heat. Cover the tagine and cook in a preheated oven, 160°C (325°F), Gas Mark 3, for 1½ hours, checking occasionally that it doesn't need more stock.

5 Remove the tagine from the oven and leave to stand for 5–10 minutes, then serve in deep dishes with the lemon wedges.

quick-fried veal with olive and lemon dressing

4 organic veal escalopes, about 150 g
   (5 oz) each
3 tablespoons plain flour
½ tablespoon paprika
3 tablespoons extra virgin olive oil
2 lemons
100 g (3½ oz) queen green olives, sliced
3–4 tablespoons chopped chervil, plus
   extra to serve
salt and pepper

To serve:
thick ribbon pasta
circles of lemon rind, boiled to soften
   (optional)

Serves 4
Preparation time: 10 minutes
Cooking time: 5–8 minutes

1 Put the veal escalopes between 2 sheets of clingfilm and beat as thinly as possible, using a rolling pin or a meat mallet. Mix the flour with the paprika, season well with salt and pepper, then dust each escalope lightly in the seasoned flour.

2 Place a large frying pan over a moderately high heat and pour in 2 tablespoons of the olive oil. Add the veal escalopes and cook quickly for about 1 minute on each side so that they are golden and crispy. If your pan is not big enough, you may have to use 2 pans or cook the veal in 2 batches.

3 Place the escalopes in a dish to keep warm and reduce the heat to moderately low. Squeeze the juice of 1 lemon into the pan with the remaining olive oil and stir with a wooden spatula to scrape off any stickiness. Cut the remaining lemon into slices and add to the pan with the olives. Allow to bubble for a few seconds, then remove the pan from the heat and sprinkle over the chervil.

4 Place the veal escalopes on warm plates and pour over the juices from the pan. Serve immediately with freshly cooked, thick ribbon pasta, and circles of lemon rind if using, and sprinkled with chopped chervil.

crispy duck legs with mini roast potatoes

4 duck legs
1 tablespoon chopped thyme
2 teaspoons sea salt
½ teaspoon pepper
8 tablespoons extra virgin olive oil
1 frisée lettuce

Mini roast potatoes:
3 tablespoons extra virgin olive oil
2–3 thyme sprigs
750 g (1½ lb) floury potatoes, cut into
    cubes
4 garlic cloves
salt and pepper

Dressing:
3 tablespoons extra virgin olive oil
1 tablespoon shallot vinegar
1 shallot, preferably purple, very finely
    diced
¼ teaspoon Dijon mustard
pinch of sugar

Serves 4
Preparation time: 10 minutes,
    plus marinating
Cooking time: 1½ hours

*In this modern twist on the classic roast, the crisp skin of the potatoes will
complement the rich duck meat, which will have been gently flavoured by
the thyme.*

1 Rub the duck legs in the thyme, salt and pepper, cover and leave at room
temperature for about 1 hour.

2 Heat the olive oil in a shallow flameproof casserole and place the duck legs,
flesh-side down, in the oil. Transfer the casserole to a preheated oven,
190°C (375°F), Gas Mark 5, and cook for about 1½ hours until the flesh is tender,
basting occasionally.

3 To make the mini roast potatoes, put the olive oil and thyme sprigs in a bowl and
season well with salt and pepper. Add the potatoes and garlic and toss well. Tip
them into a roasting tin and roast alongside the duck for about 45 minutes until
they are golden and crispy.

4 Whisk together the dressing ingredients, toss with the frisée to coat and serve
with the crispy duck and potatoes.

mexican-rubbed roast chicken tortillas

1 large, free-range chicken, about
   2 kg (4 lb)
salt and pepper
flour tortillas, to serve

Mexican rub:
1 teaspoon chipotle chilli flakes
1 teaspoon de arbol chilli flakes
2 teaspoons dried oregano
1 teaspoon dried thyme
1 tablespoon dried red pepper flakes
1 tablespoon dried onion flakes
1 teaspoon dried garlic powder
2 tablespoons piñon nuts or pine nuts
1 teaspoon cumin seeds
1 teaspoon coriander seeds
1 teaspoon sea salt
1 pickled jalepeño pepper
2 tablespoons extra virgin olive oil
finely grated rind of 2 limes
1 tablespoon lime juice

Salsa:
1 large avocado, peeled and chopped
1 small red onion, finely chopped
75 g (3 oz) pitted black olives
2 tablespoons extra virgin olive oil
4 tablespoons lime juice
4 tomatoes, skinned, deseeded and
   diced
1 bunch of coriander, roughly chopped,
   plus extra for garnishing

Serves 4
Preparation time: 20 minutes
Cooking time: about 1¼ hours

1 To prepare the Mexican rub, place all the ingredients except the jalapeño pepper, oil and lime in a small, heavy-based frying pan over a fairly low heat and toast gently for 2–3 minutes until they begin to release a smoky aroma. Tip them into a coffee grinder and process until ground. Add the jalepeño pepper, blend to a paste and scrape into a small bowl. Pour in the olive oil and lime rind and juice and mix well.

2 Rub the paste all over the chicken, working it really well into the skin so that the entire bird is covered. Place in a good-sized roasting tin, cover with foil and roast in a preheated oven, 200°C (400°F), Gas Mark 6, for 25 minutes. Remove the foil and baste the chicken well, then return to the oven for another 40–50 minutes until the juices run clear and the skin is crispy and golden. Rest the chicken somewhere warm for 10 minutes before carving. Meanwhile, mix together all the salsa ingredients and set aside until required.

3 While the chicken is resting, heat a griddle pan until hot and place the tortillas in the pan, one at a time, for 1 minute, turning them once, until they are seared and crispy on both sides. Serve the chicken in slices with the tortillas and spoonfuls of the salsa. Garnish with a sprig of coriander.

sweet things

churros dusted with icing sugar and cinnamon

300 ml (½ pint) milk
150 ml (¼ pint) water
325 g (11 oz) plain flour, sifted twice
pinch of salt
3 large eggs, beaten
olive oil, for deep-frying
icing sugar, for dusting
cinnamon-flavoured whipped cream,
    to serve

Serves 4–6
Preparation time: 10 minutes
Cooking time: 25–28 minutes

These Spanish-style doughnuts may be served as a dessert with cinnamon-flavoured whipped cream and a latte, as suggested here, or with fresh fruit.

1 Pour the milk and water into a saucepan and bring to the boil over a moderate heat. Tip in the sifted flour and salt and beat constantly with a wooden spoon until the dough begins to form a ball.

2 Remove the pan from the heat, allow the mixture to cool slightly, then whisk in the beaten eggs a little at a time until it becomes a thick, smooth batter. Spoon into a piping bag with a wide nozzle and set aside.

3 Heat the olive oil in a wok or a large, heavy-based saucepan to 190°C (375°F) or until the dough sizzles when it is dropped into the oil.

4 Pipe lengths of batter straight into the hot oil, using a small knife to cut the dough. Leave to sizzle for 3–4 minutes until the churros are cooked and golden, then remove with a slotted spoon and drain on kitchen paper. You will need to do this in batches of about 6 at a time. Keep the cooked churros warm while you cook the remaining dough.

5 Dust the cooked churros with plenty of icing sugar and serve immediately with a latte and a bowl of cinnamon-flavoured whipped cream.

coffee walnut biscotti

2 large eggs
1 tablespoon coffee essence
1 tablespoon extra virgin olive oil
100 g (3½ oz) golden caster sugar
2 tablespoons vanilla sugar
250 g (8 oz) plain flour, sifted
1½ teaspoons baking powder
pinch of salt
125 g (4 oz) ground almonds
100 g (3½ oz) walnut halves, chopped

Makes 24–26
Preparation time: 15 minutes
Cooking time: 45–55 minutes

1 Beat together the eggs, coffee essence, olive oil and the sugars in a large bowl. In another bowl, mix together the flour, baking powder, salt and ground almonds. Gradually beat the flour mixture into the eggs to form a soft dough, working in the chopped walnuts at the end.

2 Gently knead the dough into a soft, slightly sticky ball and place it on a nonstick baking sheet. Using your hands, form the dough into a long, fat, flattened sausage shape, about 30 x 12 cm (12 x 5 inches), and bake in a preheated oven, 180°C (350°F), Gas Mark 4, for 25–30 minutes until golden.

3 Take the cake out of the oven and allow to cool for a few minutes then place it carefully on a chopping board. Reduce the oven temperature to 150°C (300°F), Gas Mark 2. Cut the cake into thin slices using a very sharp knife. Lay the slices delicately on to baking sheets and return them to the oven for 20–25 minutes until they are golden and crisp. Remove the biscotti from the oven and lift gently on to a wire rack to cool. Serve at any time of the day.

sweet oatcakes

250 g (8 oz) rolled oats
50 g (2 oz) sesame seeds
3 tablespoons poppy seeds
pinch of salt
100 ml (3½ fl oz) boiling water
2 tablespoons runny honey
7 tablespoons extra virgin olive oil

To serve:
wedge of Manchego cheese
bunch of grapes

Makes 20
Preparation time: 15 minutes
Cooking time: 15 minutes

These Spanish oatcakes make a splendid finale to a meal. Continue the Spanish theme by serving with a Spanish cheese such as Manchego and a glass of sherry.

1 Combine the rolled oats, sesame seeds, poppy seeds and a pinch of salt in a large bowl and make a well in the centre. Pour in the boiling water, honey and the olive oil and stir with a wooden spoon to form a soft dough.

2 Shape the dough into 20 balls the size of a walnut. Place them on nonstick baking sheets and flatten them with the palm of your hand to make 8 cm (3½ inch) rounds. Bake in a preheated oven, 180°C (350°F), Gas Mark 4, for about 15 minutes until golden.

3 Remove the oatcakes from the oven and transfer to a wire rack to cool. Serve with a wedge of Manchego cheese and a bunch of grapes.

chocolate cup cakes with espresso icing

Cup cakes:
175 g (6 oz) self-raising flour
1 teaspoon bicarbonate of soda
2 tablespoons cocoa powder
150 g (5 oz) caster sugar
2 large eggs
150 ml (¼ pint) extra virgin olive oil
100 ml (3½ fl oz) milk
50 ml (2 fl oz) strong espresso-style
   coffee
2–3 drops coffee essence
2 tablespoons golden syrup
chocolate-covered coffee beans,
   to decorate

Espresso icing:
100 ml (3½ fl oz) double cream
2 tablespoons strong espresso-style
   coffee
2–3 drops coffee essence
150 g (5 oz) good-quality dark
   chocolate, broken into small pieces
2 tablespoons icing sugar

Makes 12
Preparation time: 15 minutes
Cooking time: 30 minutes

1 Sift the flour, bicarbonate of soda and cocoa powder into a large bowl with the sugar. In a jug or separate bowl, blend the remaining ingredients. Pour the liquid ingredients into the dry ones and beat until the mixture forms a smooth batter.

2 Pour the batter evenly into 12 paper muffin cases in a muffin tin and bake in a preheated oven, 180°C (350°F), Gas Mark 4, for about 25 minutes until the cup cakes are risen and firm to the touch. Cool on a wire rack.

3 To make the icing, put the cream in a small saucepan with the coffee and coffee essence and bring to the boil. Remove the pan from the heat and whisk in the chocolate pieces until they have melted. Beat in the icing sugar until the mixture has a thick icing consistency.

4 When the cup cakes are cold, spread them with the icing and put a chocolate-covered coffee bean in the centre of each one.

sweet orange flower water and honey baklava

Syrup:
300 g (10 oz) caster sugar
250 ml (8 fl oz) water
50 ml (2 fl oz) extra virgin olive oil
50 ml (2 fl oz) orange flower water
finely pared rind of 1 lemon
3 tablespoons clear Greek honey
1 cinnamon stick

250 g (8 oz) blanched almonds
150 g (5 oz) blanched hazelnuts
75 g (3 oz) caster sugar
150 g (5 oz) butter
50 ml (2 fl oz) extra virgin olive oil
300 g (10 oz) filo pastry (22 sheets),
    trimmed slightly to fit the tin

Makes about 20 pieces
Preparation time: 40 minutes,
    plus cooling
Cooking time: 1 hour

A typical Greek dish, baklava is famous for its delicate layers. It is usually eaten as a snack with Greek coffee, which cuts through the sweetness of the syrup.

1 Combine all the syrup ingredients in a small saucepan and heat very gently until the sugar has completely dissolved, stirring occasionally. Increase the heat slightly and leave the syrup to bubble gently, without stirring, for about 20 minutes until it forms a light, sticky syrup. Remove the pan from the heat and allow the syrup to cool in the pan. Cover the pan and chill in the refrigerator, without straining.

2 Tip the almonds and hazelnuts into a food processor, add the sugar and pulse until they are chopped but not ground.

3 Melt the butter with the olive oil in a small saucepan over a low heat, then brush generously over a piece of filo pastry, keeping the remaining pastry covered with a damp tea towel. Butter a 20 x 30 x 5 cm (8 x 12 x 2½ inch) tin, then line it with the sheet of pastry. Trim the pastry to fit the tin, leaving a few extra millimetres to allow room for the pastry to shrink during cooking. Repeat the process using 4 more sheets of pastry, brushing them with the butter and oil mixture as you layer them.

4 Scatter the pastry with one-third of the nuts and cover them with 5 more sheets of pastry, brushing them with the butter and oil mixture as you go. Add half the remaining nuts and then cover them with 5 more sheets of pastry, the remaining nuts and then the remaining 7 sheets of pastry.

5 Brush the top of the baklava liberally with the remaining butter/oil mixture. Use a sharp knife to cut through the top few layers of pastry in a criss-cross pattern so that you have about 20 diamond shapes. Bake in a preheated oven, 190°C (375°F), Gas Mark 5, for about 40 minutes until golden.

6 Remove the cinnamon stick and lemon rind from the syrup. As soon as you take the baklava from the oven, pour the syrup evenly over it. Leave to cool, then cut into the scored diamond shapes. Serve with Greek coffee.

wild strawberries and clotted cream crêpes

375 g (12 oz) fresh wild strawberries

2 tablespoons aged balsamic vinegar

1 tablespoon golden caster sugar

2 tablespoons Mandarin and Lemon Oil
(see page 19)

125 g (4 oz) plain flour, sifted

pinch of salt

2 eggs, lightly beaten

300 ml (½ pint) semi-skimmed milk

25 g (1 oz) butter, melted

olive oil, for frying

thick clotted cream, to serve

Serves 4

Preparation time: 12 minutes,
plus macerating

Cooking time: 16–25 minutes

Strawberries and balsamic vinegar make a surprisingly delicious partnership. The infused mandarin and lemon olive oil will add an extra depth to the crêpes, making this the perfect summer dessert.

1 Halve the strawberries, put them in a bowl and pour over the balsamic vinegar, sugar and 1 tablespoon of the mandarin and lemon oil. Stir to combine and leave to macerate for 1 hour.

2 To make the crêpe batter, combine the flour and salt in a large bowl. Make a well in the centre and pour in the beaten eggs and milk. Whisk them, gradually incorporating all the flour from the side of the bowl, until you have a smooth and lump-free batter. Whisk in the melted butter and the remaining mandarin and lemon oil and pour into a measuring jug.

3 Heat 1 teaspoon of olive oil in a crêpe pan until hot, then carefully wipe away most of it with kitchen paper. Pour in just enough batter to coat the base when you shake the pan. Cook over a moderate heat for 1–2 minutes until bubbles start appearing in the batter, then flip the crêpe with a palette knife, or a flip of the wrist if you're feeling confident. Cook the other side until golden, then tip the crêpe directly on to greaseproof paper and keep warm. Repeat this process with the remaining batter – you should be able to make 8 crêpes.

4 To serve, spoon some of the strawberry mixture on to the centre of a crêpe, fold it in half and place on a warm serving dish. Drizzle with some of the strawberry juices and add a dollop of clotted cream. Serve immediately.

pistachio, lemon and polenta cake with rosewater syrup

125 g (4 oz) plain flour

150 g (5 oz) polenta flour

200 g (7 oz) caster sugar

1 teaspoon baking powder

150 ml (¼ pint) olive oil

250 g (8 oz) full-fat yogurt

3 eggs

2 tablespoons rosewater

finely grated rind of 2 lemons and
    their juice

75 g (3 oz) pistachios, roughly chopped

Greek yogurt, to serve

Rosewater syrup:

100 g (3½ oz) caster sugar

1 tablespoon rosewater

100 ml (3½ fl oz) water

rind of 1 lemon, pared in strips with
    a vegetable peeler

Serves 6–8

Preparation time: 20 minutes

Cooking time: about 1½ hours

1 Combine the flours, sugar and baking powder in a large bowl. In a separate bowl, whisk the olive oil with the yogurt, eggs and rosewater. Pour the wet ingredients into the dry ones and beat with a wooden spoon until smooth. Stir in the lemon rind and juice and 50 g (2 oz) of the chopped pistachios. Pour into a 23 cm (9 inch) spring-form cake tin, base-lined with greaseproof paper, and bake in a preheated oven, 150°C (300°F), Gas Mark 2, for about 1½ hours until golden and firm.

2 Meanwhile, put all the syrup ingredients in a small saucepan and heat very gently until the sugar has completely dissolved, stirring occasionally. Increase the heat slightly and leave the syrup to bubble gently, without stirring, for about 12 minutes until it forms a light syrup. Leave to cool, then shred the lemon peel very thinly.

3 Remove the cake from the oven and leave to cool for about 10 minutes. Scatter the cake with the remaining pistachios and the shredded lemon peel and pour half the cool syrup evenly over the top. Leave to cool completely still in the tin, then remove the cake and cut it into 6–8 wedges. Serve drizzled with the remaining syrup and a dollop of Greek yogurt.

chocolate, almond and fig tart

100 g (3½ oz) butter

50 g (2 oz) sugar

3 egg yolks

2 tablespoons extra virgin olive oil

200 g (7 oz) plain flour, sifted, plus extra
for dusting

50g (2 oz) ground almonds

crème fraîche, to serve

Filling:

150 g (5 oz) good-quality dark chocolate

1 tablespoon cocoa powder, plus extra
for dusting

pinch of salt

75 g (3 oz) butter

2 tablespoons extra virgin olive oil

2 large egg yolks, plus 3 large eggs

150 g (5 oz) caster sugar

50 ml (2 fl oz) double cream

2 tablespoons Amaretto di Saronno
liqueur

3 fresh figs, halved

1 tablespoon flaked almonds, toasted

Serves 6–8

Preparation time: 30 minutes,
plus chilling

Cooking time: about 1 hour

It's important to buy a really good-quality chocolate for this tart (at least 70 per cent cocoa solids) as it will make all the difference to the taste. The tart is rich and dense, so you'll need to serve only a small slice per person.

1 To make the pastry, beat together the butter and sugar until pale, then beat in the egg yolks and olive oil. Mix in the flour and ground almonds and work together until you have a soft dough. Wrap loosely in clingfilm and chill in the refrigerator for 1 hour.

2 Roll out the dough on a lightly floured board until it is slightly bigger than a 23 cm (9 inch) fluted tart tin. Lift the dough into the tin, pressing it gently so that it rises up the sides. Cover and chill in the refrigerator for 30 minutes.

3 Cover the base of the tart with greaseproof paper and fill it with baking beans. Bake blind in a preheated oven, 180°C (350°F), Gas Mark 4, for 15 minutes. Remove the paper and beans and return the pastry to the oven for a further 5 minutes until it is crisp and lightly golden. Remove the pastry case but leave the oven on.

4 To make the filling, put the chocolate, cocoa powder, salt, butter and olive oil in a heatproof bowl set over a pan of barely simmering water and leave to melt slowly. Remove the pan and allow the melted chocolate to cool slightly. In a separate bowl, beat together the egg yolks, eggs and sugar until pale and thick.

5 Fold the chocolate into the egg mixture and stir in the double cream and Amaretto. Pour the mixture into the pastry case and arrange the halved figs on the top. Sprinkle with the flaked almonds, then return the tart to the oven for 30–35 minutes until just set.

6 Remove the tart from the oven and allow to cool slightly. Serve warm, dusted with cocoa powder and with a dollop of crème fraîche.

mini chocolate and cardamom pots

8–10 cardamom pods
200 g (7 oz) very good-quality dark
　chocolate, broken into squares
2 tablespoons coffee liqueur
2 tablespoons extra virgin olive oil
3 large eggs, separated

To serve:
whipped cream
coffee-flavoured chocolates

Serves 4
Preparation time: 12 minutes,
　plus chilling
Cooking time: 8 minutes

This quick and easy dessert looks wonderfully decadent and tastes divine. The cardamom pods add an unusual twist, while the coffee liqueur gives it a bit of an alcoholic kick.

1 Remove the cardamom seeds from their pods and crush to a powder using a pestle and mortar.

2 Place the chocolate squares in a small, heatproof bowl with the ground cardamom, coffee liqueur and olive oil and set over a pan of barely simmering water. Leave the chocolate to melt very slowly without stirring for about 8 minutes.

3 Remove the bowl of chocolate from the heat and quickly beat in the egg yolks. Set aside while you put the egg whites in a large bowl and whisk until stiff. Stir 1 tablespoon of the beaten eggs into the chocolate mixture to slacken it, then carefully fold in the remaining egg whites with a metal spoon.

4 Divide the mixture among 4 ramekins. Cover and chill in the refrigerator for about 2 hours until set, then serve with a little whipped cream and some crushed coffee-flavoured chocolates.

orange and ginger crisp gelato

Orange and ginger crisps:
4 tablespoons caster sugar
4 tablespoons golden syrup
1½ tablespoons orange oil, plus extra
    for greasing
50 g (2 oz) butter
6 tablespoons plain flour, sifted
2 teaspoons ground ginger
finely grated rind of 1 orange

Gelato:
500 ml (17 fl oz) double cream
finely grated rind of 2 oranges
juice of 1 orange
3 large egg yolks
75 g (3 oz) golden caster sugar
75 ml (3 fl oz) extra virgin olive oil

Serves 4
Preparation time: 25 minutes, plus
    chilling and freezing
Cooking time: about 25 minutes

1 To make the crisps, put the sugar, golden syrup, orange oil and butter in a saucepan over a low heat and allow the sugar to dissolve slowly. When the sugar has dissolved and the mixture begins to boil, remove the pan from the heat and stir in the flour, ginger and orange rind.

2 Use a teaspoon to dollop the mixture on to 2 large, nonstick baking sheets, lightly greased with orange oil, placing about 4 biscuits on each sheet. Spread them out a little with the back of the spoon and bake in a preheated oven, 200°C (400°F), Gas Mark 6, for about 10 minutes until golden. When they are cool enough to handle, transfer with a palette knife to a wire rack to cool completely. You will need to cook the crisps in 2 batches.

3 To make the gelato, pour the cream into a saucepan with the orange rind and juice and bring to the boil. Remove the pan from the heat. Using an electric hand whisk, beat the egg yolks and sugar in a bowl for about 5 minutes until the eggs are thick and creamy and have tripled in volume. Reduce the speed and slowly trickle in the olive oil, beating until it is well combined. Now gradually beat the hot cream into the eggs, then return the mixture to the pan. Place the pan over a moderately low heat and stir constantly with a wooden spoon until the mixture thickens. It should be thick enough to coat the back of the spoon, but be careful not to let it boil. Remove the pan from the heat and allow to cool. When the gelato is cold, cover and chill in the refrigerator for 1–2 hours.

4 Transfer the gelato to an ice-cream machine and freeze according to the manufacturer's instructions. Crumble 12 of the crisps into the gelato, put it into a freezerproof container and freeze for at least 2 hours until completely frozen. Serve the gelato with the remaining biscuits.

index

acknowledgments

Executive Editor Sarah Ford
Editor Charlotte Wilson
Executive Art Editor Geoff Fennell
Photographer Gus Filgate
Food Stylist David Morgan

Stylist Rachel Jukes
Senior Production Controller Manjit Sihra
Picture Researcher Jennifer Veall